COLORADO BED & BREAKFAST COOKBOOK

Happy Cooking!

Carol Faino

1999

Published by
PEPPERMINT PRESS
PO Box 370235
Denver, CO 80237-0235
Email: bbcookbook@aol.com
Website: www.bbcookbook.com

1st Printing	September 1996	5,000 copies
2nd Printing	December 1996	10,000 copies
3rd Printing	November 1997	5,000 copies
4th Printing	October 1998	5,000 copies
5th Printing	July 1999	5,000 copies

Cover Design: SYKES DESIGN GRAPHICS & LAURA GEPPINGER
                 Estes Park, Colorado
Cover Photos: JAMES FRANK
                 Estes Park, Colorado
Cover Location: ROMANTIC RIVERSONG INN
                 Estes Park, Colorado
Cover Food: JAN JACKSON, MANAGER/CHEF
                 Romantic RiverSong Inn
                 Estes Park, Colorado

ISBN 0-9653751-8-8

Printed in the USA by
WIMMER
The Wimmer Companies
Memphis
1-800-548-2537

To my parents,
who, by their example,
have given me the recipe
for a happy, healthy
and meaningful life.

Acknowledgements

Creating a book is a work involving many people. We owe a great deal of gratitude to the following friends, family members and business colleagues for their support, inspiration, enthusiasm, time and talents:

Gary Enright, Linda Faino, Gordon McCollum, Laurel Merkwan, our friends at Children's Book Place, Jim Baez, Dave Lane, Susie Aikman, Jennifer Merkwan Anderson, Rick and Linda Ribbentrop, Kirk Collins, Susan John, Teresa Gonzalez, Sandy Gander and friends at UDC, AHA Staff of Colorado and Wyoming, our official taste testers, and a special thank you to the owners, innkeepers and chefs of the 85 Colorado bed and breakfasts who generously shared their recipes and helped make our dream come true.

We want to express our love and heartfelt thanks to our parents, Margaret and Harold McCollum and Nan and Lawrence Kaitfors; our husbands, Rod Faino and Don Hazledine; and children, Kyle, Erin and Ryan Faino for their continuous support and encouragement.

Table of Contents

Introduction

My husband Rod and I had our first bed and breakfast experience a few years ago in Victoria, British Columbia. Our hosts were delightful, our room was charming, breakfast was truly memorable, and when we said our thank yous and goodbyes, the owners presented us with a keepsake – a pen and ink drawing of their inn. Needless to say, we were hooked! We have stayed in many B&B's since and even dream of someday having our own.

Combining my enchantment with the B&B concept, my longtime interest in cooking, the generosity and enthusiasm of 85 Colorado B&B owners, the invaluable guidance of special friend and mentor, author Gary Enright, and my fortune of having such a talented and accomplished writer and willing co-author and friend in Doreen Hazledine, *Colorado Bed & Breakfast Cookbook* has become a reality.

This cookbook is a collection of recipes, ranging from the simple to the gourmet, that have received rave reviews from B&B guests. Many dishes can be made the night before serving or have shortcuts to help make entertaining easier. The recipes were home kitchen tested at an altitude of 5,920 feet, taste tested and edited for clarity.

I encourage you to have fun in the kitchen, be adventurous and even try ingredients that are new and unfamiliar to you. The next time you feel like entertaining, why not delight your friends by inviting them for breakfast or brunch instead of the usual dinner. If you particularly enjoy a recipe from this book, I know the B&B owners would love to hear from you. Send them a postcard; or better yet, pick up the phone and make a reservation! Innkeepers are some of the friendliest and most interesting people you will ever meet, and they certainly know how to serve food with flair!

Doreen and I have researched and compiled B&B information and recipes with care, so that you will have a cookbook and guide that is as reliable and accurate as possible. We hope you find this book both interesting and useful. Enjoy *Colorado Bed & Breakfast Cookbook.*

Carol Faino
Denver, Colorado
August 1996

BREADS
&
MUFFINS

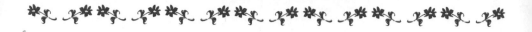

The Tudor Rose

The Tudor Rose is a stately, country manor located high on a piñon hill. The land surrounding this unique Tudor estate covers 37 sprawling acres that were once part of an 1890's homestead.

Remnants of the old homestead buildings and a hand-dug, stone-lined well still stand in the lower pasture, defiant of the passage of time.

INNKEEPERS:	*Jon & Terre' Terrell*
ADDRESS:	*6720 Paradise Road; PO Box 89*
	Salida, CO 81201
TELEPHONE:	*(719) 539-2002; (800) 379-0889*
ROOMS:	*4 Rooms; 2 Suites; Private & shared baths*
OPEN:	*Year-round*
CHILDREN:	*6 years and older welcome*
ANIMALS:	*Welcome; Fenced outdoor accommodations;*
	Overnight stabling
SMOKING:	*Non-smoking in house and barn*

Chocolate Bread
with Raspberry Sauce

2 1/2 c. flour
1 1/2 t. baking soda
1/2 c. cocoa
1 c. sugar
1/2 t. salt
1 egg, beaten
1/3 c. butter, melted
1 1/4 c. sour milk (see note below)
3/4 c. walnuts, chopped
Smucker's natural red raspberry syrup
Red raspberries, fresh

In a large bowl, sift together the first 5 ingredients. In a smaller bowl, combine the egg, melted butter and sour milk. Add the wet ingredients to the dry ingredients and stir just until blended. Fold in the nuts. Pour batter into a greased 9x5-inch loaf pan. Bake at 350° F. for 50-60 minutes, or until toothpick inserted comes out clean. Do not overbake.

Note: To make sour milk, put 1 tablespoon vinegar in a measuring cup, add enough milk (at room temperature) to make 1 1/4 cups. Allow mixture to sit for 5 minutes.

Presentation: Place a piece of warm bread on a small plate. Drizzle Smucker's natural red raspberry syrup over bread and around plate. Garnish with fresh red raspberries.

Carol's Corner
This is perfect for a special breakfast. Or top the bread with a big scoop of vanilla ice cream before adding the syrup and raspberries, and it becomes a beautiful, memorable dessert.

Ambiance Inn

The Ambiance Inn is internationally recognized as one of the finest bed and breakfasts in the Rocky Mountain region. Set in pastoral Carbondale, half a block off Main Street, the inn is a contemporary chalet with spacious, comfortable rooms.

Year-round activities, just minutes away from the inn, include Gold Medal fishing, white water rafting, golf, horseback riding, cross-country and alpine skiing.

INNKEEPERS:	*Bob & Norma Morris*
ADDRESS:	*66 N. Second Street; Carbondale, CO 81623*
	PO Box 10932; Aspen, CO 81612
TELEPHONE:	*(970) 963-3597; (800) 350-1515*
ROOMS:	*4 Rooms; Private baths*
OPEN:	*Year-round*
CHILDREN:	*No restrictions*
ANIMALS:	*Extra charge for pets*
SMOKING:	*Restricted areas only*

Poppy Seed Bread

2 c. sugar
1 1/2 c. vegetable oil
3 eggs
1 1/2 t. vanilla extract
1 1/2 t. almond extract
3 c. flour
1/2 t. salt
1 1/2 t. baking powder
2 T. poppy seeds
1 1/2 c. milk
Glaze (recipe below)

Cream together the sugar, oil, eggs, and vanilla and almond extracts in a large bowl. Combine the flour, salt, baking powder and poppy seeds in a separate bowl. Add the dry ingredients to the sugar mixture alternately with the milk, ending with the dry ingredients. Stir just until ingredients are combined. Do not overmix. Bake in two greased and floured 9x5-inch loaf pans at 350° F. for approximately 1 hour, or until a toothpick inserted comes out clean. While the bread is still warm and in the pan, drizzle the glaze over the top of the loaves. Place on a wire rack until almost cool. Run a knife around the edges of the pans and remove the loaves. Finish cooling on a wire rack.

Glaze
1/4 cup orange juice
3/4 cup sugar
1/2 teaspoon almond extract

Combine the orange juice, sugar and almond extract. Drizzle over the warm loaves of bread.

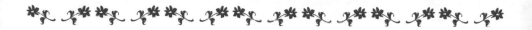

Dripping Springs Inn

Dripping Springs Inn is a unique country inn located in the Roosevelt National Forest on the Big Thompson River. Seven acres of ponderosa pines and aspens, that border a horseshoe bend in the river, allow plenty of wildlife viewing for guests.

Delicious homemade breakfasts are served every morning. "Burrrrp," one guest commented, "What a wonderful breakfast! As far as baking, Betty Crocker don't have a thing on you all!"

INNKEEPERS: *Oliver & Janie Robertson*
ADDRESS: *2551 Highway 34*
Drake, CO 80515 (Estes Park)
TELEPHONE: *(970) 586-3406*
ROOMS: *9 Rooms; Private and shared baths*
OPEN: *Year-round*
CHILDREN: *Prohibited*
ANIMALS: *Prohibited; Resident pets*
SMOKING: *Prohibited*

Bread Pudding Bread

10 c. bread, approximately, torn into bite-size pieces (see note below)
1 c. raisins
1 t. cinnamon
1/2 c. nuts
1 c. sugar
3 eggs
1 c. milk
1 t. vanilla

Pile the pieces of bread into a 9x5-inch loaf pan until the bread is about 2 inches above the rim of the pan. This step determines the correct quantity of bread needed. Then dump the bread pieces into a large bowl. In a small bowl, combine the raisins, cinnamon and nuts. Add to the bread. Mix together the sugar, eggs, milk and vanilla and pour over the bread mixture. Mix until all the bread is wet. If you need more liquid, just add a little more milk. Pack the mixture into the loaf pan. It will now be about 1 inch below the rim of the pan. It can be refrigerated until ready to bake, or it can be baked immediately. Bake at 350° F. for about 1 hour. Cool about 10-15 minutes and remove from pan. Finish cooling on a wire rack and refrigerate. The bread tastes and slices best when cold or at room temperature.

Note: Leftover French bread, croissants, muffins, etc. work well.

"So different...plain old bread pudding baked in a loaf pan and sliced. My guests rave about this and it is just leftover bread!"
Janie Robertson – Dripping Springs B&B Inn

Woodland Inn

W oodland Inn is a cozy country inn nestled in the foothills of majestic Pikes Peak. Surrounded by 12 private acres of aspen and fir trees, the Woodland Inn is conveniently located just minutes from Colorado Springs and Manitou Springs in beautiful Woodland Park, truly "The City Above the Clouds."

Hot air balloon flights can be arranged for a morning of adventure. "A special unexpected treasure!" one guest commented, "We'll remember this forever."

INNKEEPERS: *Frank & Nancy O'Neil*
ADDRESS: *159 Trull Road*
Woodland Park, CO 80863
TELEPHONE: *(719) 687-8209; (800) 226-9565*
ROOMS: *7 Rooms; All with private baths; 1 Room available for disabled persons*
OPEN: *Year-round*
CHILDREN: *Welcome*
ANIMALS: *Cat and dog live on premises*
SMOKING: *Outside only*

Tomato Soup Cake

3 T. shortening
1 large or 2 small eggs
1 c. sugar
1 t. baking soda
1 can tomato soup
1 1/2 c. flour
2 t. baking powder
1/2 t. salt
1 t. cinnamon
1/2 t. ground cloves
1 c. raisins
1/2 c. chopped walnuts, optional

*х*Carol's Corner
My son Kyle says this spice bread is <u>*so*</u> *good, he often eats it straight from the freezer.*

Cream shortening, eggs and sugar. Stir baking soda into the can of soup and watch the reaction! Add to the creamed mixture. Stir in the sifted flour, baking powder, salt and spices. Then add raisins and nuts. Pour into a greased 9x5-inch loaf pan.   Bake at 350° F. for approximately 40-45 minutes. Cool about an hour and then remove from pan by turning upside down into the palm of your hand. Wrap the loaf tightly in plastic wrap. It can be sliced and served plain or topped with a thin glaze of powdered sugar and lemon juice mixed together to desired consistency.

"This recipe was my mother's. Few people have ever heard of it, and the name is less than appetizing, but the results are a moist and slightly sweet tasting bread. Great for breakfast, brunch or snacks. This bread is part of our 'Field Breakfast' when Frank takes our guests out on a morning of hot-air ballooning at South Park. This breakfast follows the flight and chase and the champagne ritual for first timers."
Nancy O'Neil – Woodland Inn B&B

Awarenest Victorian

The Awarenest Victorian Bed and Breakfast was built in 1901 for a conductor with the Denver-Rio Grande railway. It has been fully restored with authentic Victorian furnishings that include period antiques and vintage stained glass.

Located on a bicycle route that joins Colorado Springs to the historic district of Old Colorado City, Awarenest is within walking distance of quaint boutiques and charming eateries.

INNKEEPERS:	*Karla & Rex Hefferan*
ADDRESS:	*1218 West Pikes Peak Avenue*
	Colorado Springs, CO 80904
TELEPHONE:	*(719) 630-8241*
ROOMS:	*1 Suite; Attached bath*
OPEN:	*Year-round*
CHILDREN:	*Welcome*
ANIMALS:	*Prohibited; Resident pets*
SMOKING:	*Prohibited*

One Pan Banana Bread

1/3 c. vegetable oil
1 1/2 c. mashed ripe bananas
1/2 t. vanilla
3 eggs
2 2/3 c. Bisquick
1 c. sugar
1/2 c. nuts, chopped (not too fine)
1/2 c. chocolate bits (optional)

Preheat oven to 350° F. Mix all the ingredients together and bake in a greased 9x5-inch loaf pan for 55-65 minutes. Cool 5 minutes and remove from pan. Finish cooling on a wire rack.

Here in Colorado, follow high altitude adjustment as follows: Preheat oven to 375° F. Decrease Bisquick to 2 cups and sugar to 2/3 cup. Add 1/4 cup all-purpose flour. Bake for 50-55 minutes.

Carol's Corner
I tried this recipe adding the chocolate bits. The chocolate and banana flavors are a nice combination.

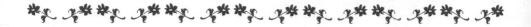

Meadow Creek

ASABATTLES

M eadow Creek, once part of the 250 acre Douglass ranch, was built
in 1929 by Prince Balthasar Gialma Odescalchi, noble of the Holy
Roman Empire. The property is nestled in a secluded meadow
surrounded by stone outcroppings. Tall pines and aspens border a small
spring-fed creek.

"We are pleased to share our little piece of God's Country."

~ Owners, Pat, Dennis, Judy & Don

INNKEEPERS:	*Pat & Dennis Carnahan; Judy & Don Otis*
ADDRESS:	*13438 US Highway 285*
	Pine, CO 80470
TELEPHONE:	*(303) 838-4167; (303) 838-4899*
ROOMS:	*5 Rooms; 2 Suites; All with private baths*
OPEN:	*Year-round*
CHILDREN:	*Discouraged; Not child-proof*
ANIMALS:	*Prohibited*
SMOKING:	*Not inside*

Pistachio Banana Bread

2 1/2 c. flour
1 1/2 c. sugar
1/2 t. salt
1/2 t. soda
2 (3.4 oz.) pkgs. pistachio instant pudding
1 c. oil
2 c. mashed ripe bananas (about 4 large)
5 eggs
1 t. vanilla

Preheat oven to 350° F. (High altitude: 375°) Combine dry ingredients. Add oil, banana, eggs and vanilla. Mix well. Prepare 2 loaf pans (9x5-inch) by cutting wax paper to fit in bottom. Then spray sides of pans with cooking spray. Bake 50-60 minutes. Remove from pans after cooling for 15 minutes. Cool completely on a wire rack. Freezes well.

Carol's Corner

This pretty, light green bread is good any time of the year, but be sure to remember it at Christmas or when you're planning your "green" menu for St. Patrick's Day. I mailed a loaf of this bread to my daughter Erin to "taste test." She took a slice of the bread to work for lunch. However, it disappeared before she had a chance to eat it. When a co-worker asked her for the recipe, the mystery was solved.

Apple Avenue

A pple Avenue Bed and Breakfast offers friendly service and pleasant accommodations in Loveland, Colorado, home to many artists, sculptors and foundries. Public sculpture is found throughout the city, with an impressive collection at Benson Park, an easy walk from Apple Avenue Bed and Breakfast.

Owner Tom Harroun is a retired IBM engineer. Ann Harroun, owner, is a former Vermont State Legislator and political junkie.

INNKEEPERS:	*Tom & Ann Harroun*
ADDRESS:	*3321 Apple Avenue*
	Loveland, CO 80538
TELEPHONE:	*(970) 667-2665*
ROOMS:	*2 Rooms; 1 1/2 baths*
OPEN:	*Year-round*
CHILDREN:	*Welcome*
ANIMALS:	*Prohibited*
SMOKING:	*Prohibited*

Orange-Date-Nut Muffins

2 c. flour
2 t. baking powder
1/2 t. salt
1/2 c. sugar
1 c. dates, chopped
1/2 c. walnuts, chopped
2 t. orange peel
2/3 c. canola oil
3/4 c. orange juice
1 t. orange extract
2 eggs, beaten

> ✻Carol's Corner
> *This is a great tasting, moist muffin...bursting with flavor and texture!*

Sift together the flour, baking powder, salt and sugar. Set aside. In a small bowl, mix together the dates, nuts and orange peel. Set aside. In a large bowl, beat together the oil, orange juice, orange extract and eggs. Then add the sifted dry ingredients all at once and stir just until moistened. Gently fold in the dates, nuts and orange peel. Spoon batter into greased and floured muffin tins. Bake at 375° F. for approximately 15-20 minutes, or until lightly brown on top. Makes 18 muffins.

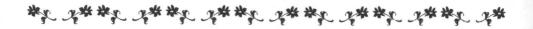

Country Gardens

C harmingly furnished with antiques, including an 1897 piano and a working 1903 victrola, Country Gardens Bed and Breakfast was custom built in 1979 with the idea to create a country/Victorian atmosphere.

A covered porch wraps around three sides of the house and features a comfortable swing and various sitting areas. Guests stroll through the four acres of gardens and trees or relax in the large Victorian gazebo.

INNKEEPERS:	*Arlie & Donna Munsie*
ADDRESS:	*1619 E. 136th Avenue; PO Box 33765*
	Northglenn, CO 80233
TELEPHONE:	*(303) 451-1724; (800) 475-1724*
ROOMS:	*4 Rooms; Private baths*
OPEN:	*Year-round*
CHILDREN:	*12 and older are welcome*
ANIMALS:	*Prohibited*
SMOKING:	*Prohibited*

Pineapple Bran Muffins

2 1/2 c. flour
1 1/2 c. sugar
2 1/2 t. baking soda
1 t. salt
1/2 t. cinnamon
1/4 t. allspice
2 1/2 c. bran cereal of choice
2 eggs, beaten
2 c. buttermilk
1/2 c. oil
1 (7 1/2 oz.) can crushed pineapple, undrained

Carol's Corner

For the 2 1/2 cups cereal called for in the recipe, Donna at Country Gardens suggests using 1 1/2 cups Mueslix with raisins, almonds and dates and 1 cup Raisin Bran cereal.

In a very large bowl, sift together the flour, sugar, baking soda, salt, cinnamon and allspice. Mix in cereal. In a smaller bowl, combine eggs, buttermilk, oil and pineapple. Add to dry ingredients and stir just until combined. Pour batter into paper baking cups or greased muffin tins. Bake at 400° F. for approximately 15-20 minutes. Makes about 24 muffins.

Flynn's Inn

F lynn's Inn is located just one block from Colorado State University and is only a five-minute walk to Historic Old Town in Fort Collins, Colorado. This turn-of-the-century house has spacious common areas, including living room, dining room, sun room and a backyard with a waterfall and pond that encourage B & B camaraderie.

Flynn's Inn is a welcome retreat in lovely Fort Collins, Colorado.

INNKEEPERS:	*Colleen & Carie Conway*
ADDRESS:	*700 Remington*
	Fort Collins, CO 80524
TELEPHONE:	*(970) 484-9984*
ROOMS:	*3 Rooms; Private and shared baths*
OPEN:	*Year-round*
CHILDREN:	*Can't accommodate children under 10*
ANIMALS:	*Prohibited*
SMOKING:	*Prohibited in house; Smoking areas provided on porch and in backyard*

Blueberry Cream Muffins

4 eggs
2 c. sugar
1 c. oil
1 t. vanilla
4 c. flour
1 t. salt
1 t. baking soda
2 t. baking powder
2 c. sour cream
2 c. fresh blueberries

Beat eggs and slowly add sugar. While beating, slowly add oil and vanilla. Mix dry ingredients and add alternately with sour cream to the egg mixture. Gently fold in blueberries.   Spoon batter into greased and floured muffin tins or use paper liners.   Bake at 400° F. for about 20 minutes. Makes 24 muffins.

Note: The blueberry muffins are outstanding when you have access to fresh blueberries. If you must use frozen berries, do not let them thaw first. Add 5 to 8 minutes to the baking time.

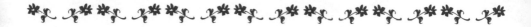

The Queen Anne

Elegance and history combine in two, side-by-side Victorians in downtown Denver that is known as The Queen Anne Bed and Breakfast Inn. Special features include a grand oak staircase, rare 35-foot turret, antiques, art and flowers that showcase the warm hospitality for which the West, Denver and this inn are well known.

The Queen Anne was the first urban bed and breakfast inn in Denver.

INNKEEPERS:	*Tom King*
ADDRESS:	*2147-51 Tremont Place*
	Denver, CO 80205
TELEPHONE:	*(303) 296-6666; (800) 432-INNS*
ROOMS:	*4 Two-Bedroom Suites; 10 Double Rooms; All with private baths*
OPEN:	*Year-round*
CHILDREN:	*Welcome*
ANIMALS:	*Prohibited*
SMOKING:	*Prohibited*

Lemony Orange Muffins

1 c. sugar
2/3 c. shortening
2 eggs
2 T. freshly squeezed lemon juice
3 c. all-purpose flour
3 t. baking powder
1/2 t. salt
1 t. ground nutmeg
1 c. milk
Orange Glaze (recipe below)
Orange Butter (recipe below)

In a large bowl, cream together sugar, shortening, eggs and lemon juice. Sift together flour, baking powder, salt and nutmeg. Add to creamed mixture alternately with milk. Stir with spoon. Do not overmix. Fill greased or paper lined muffin pans 1/2 to 2/3 full. Bake at 350° F. for approximately 20-25 minutes. Brush muffins with Orange Glaze while still warm. Let muffins cool. Serve with Orange Butter. Makes 24 muffins.

<u>Orange Glaze</u>
1 1/2 c. powdered sugar
3-4 T. freshly squeezed orange juice
2 T. grated orange zest (will probably need 2 oranges)

<u>Orange Butter</u>
3 T. powdered sugar
2 T. grated orange zest (will probably need 2 oranges)
1/2 c. unsalted butter, softened

Steamboat Valley Guest House

Built on Crawford Hill in 1957 with logs from the town mill and bricks from the old flour mill, Steamboat Valley Guest House was the Yampa Valley College president's residence in the 1960's. It was remodeled as a bed and breakfast in 1993.

The Guest House is within easy walking distance of the Old Town shops and restaurants and features covered parking, ski and bike storage and an outdoor hot tub.

INNKEEPERS:	*Alice & George Lund*
ADDRESS:	*1245 Crawford Avenue; PO Box 773815*
	Steamboat Springs, CO 80477
TELEPHONE:	*(970) 870-9017; (800) 530-3866*
ROOMS:	*3 Rooms; 1 Suite; All with private baths*
OPEN:	*Year-round*
CHILDREN:	*Accommodations not suitable for young children*
ANIMALS:	*Prohibited*
SMOKING:	*Prohibited*

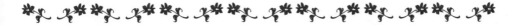

Ice Box
English Tea Muffins

1/2 c. butter
3/4 c. sugar
1 egg
1/2 t. salt
1/4 t. ground cinnamon
2 t. baking powder
2 c. flour
1 c. milk
3/4 c. currants

Topping
1/2 c. brown sugar
1/4 c. chopped pecans
1 t. ground cinnamon

Preheat oven to 350° F. Cream butter and sugar. Add egg and blend well. In a separate bowl, combine salt, cinnamon, baking powder and flour; add alternately with milk to the creamed mixture. Stir in currants. Spoon into greased muffin cups about 3/4 full. Combine topping ingredients and sprinkle on muffins. Press topping in slightly. Bake for 20-25 minutes. Makes 12 muffins.

Make-ahead tip: Batter may be covered tightly and stored in refrigerator for 2-3 weeks.

The Thomas House

The Thomas House Bed and Breakfast was built in 1888 as a rooming house for the bustling business brought by the Denver and Rio Grande Railroad. Railroad workers flocked to Salida, which became a major intersection for narrow and standard gauge rail.

Driving into Chaffee County and Salida, a sign says, "Now This is Colorado." With more warmth and sunshine, world famous river rapids and more 14,000 ft. peaks than any other county in Colorado, the slogan is certainly not an overstatement.

INNKEEPERS:	*Tammy & Steve Office*
ADDRESS:	*307 East First Street*
	Salida, CO 81201
TELEPHONE:	*(719) 539-7104; (888) 228-1410*
ROOMS:	*4 Rooms; 1 Suite; All with private baths*
OPEN:	*Year-round*
CHILDREN:	*Welcome*
ANIMALS:	*Prohibited*
SMOKING:	*Prohibited*

Six-Week Raisin Bran Muffins

5 c. flour
5 t. baking soda
2 t. salt
1 t. cinnamon
1/2 t. allspice
3 c. sugar
12 oz. raisin bran cereal
4 c. (1 qt.) buttermilk
4 eggs, beaten
1 c. vegetable oil

"This recipe has been a savior when dealing with an especially large or small (more than 12 or less than 4) breakfast crowd. You don't have to think very clearly in the morning to get great results every time, and you can make only the number of muffins you need, so there is little waste."
Tammy Office – Thomas House B&B

Topping
1 c. sugar
1 t. cinnamon

In a <u>very</u> large bowl, mix together the flour, baking soda, salt, spices, sugar and cereal. Add buttermilk, eggs and oil. Mix thoroughly.

Make-ahead tip: At this point you may transfer the batter to a large airtight container and refrigerate for up to 6 weeks.

When ready to bake, preheat oven to 375° F. Fill greased and floured muffin cups 3/4 full and bake 20-25 minutes or until a toothpick comes out clean. Remove from pan immediately and dip the tops of muffins into cinnamon-sugar mixture. Best when served warm.

Note: This recipe makes a large quantity. If desired, cut recipe in half.

Thompson House Inn

B uilt in 1887, the Thompson House Inn is a historic landmark and
former home of J.B. Thompson, Longmont's first hardware
merchant. Thompson was one of the "Chicago Colonists" who settled in
the St. Vrain Valley in the late 19th century.

Victorian luxury has been combined with contemporary conveniences to
provide the most modern bed and breakfast amenities. Guests relax in a
beautiful parlor that includes such features as inlaid wood floors, high
ceilings, original wood moldings and a lovely black marble fireplace.

INNKEEPERS:	*Sheila Merrill & Marvin Bonta*
ADDRESS:	*537 Terry Street*
	Longmont, CO 80501
TELEPHONE:	*(303) 651-6675*
ROOMS:	*7 Rooms; All with private baths*
OPEN:	*Year-round*
CHILDREN:	*Children welcome over the age of 10*
ANIMALS:	*Prohibited*
SMOKING:	*Smoking in outdoor areas only*

Lemon Ginger Poppy Seed Muffins

2 c. flour
1 t. baking soda
1/4 c. poppy seeds
1 c. sugar
Zest from 1 lemon
2 T. peeled and chopped fresh ginger
1/2 c. (1 stick) butter
2 eggs
1 c. buttermilk or plain yogurt

Mix together the flour, baking soda and poppy seeds. Set aside. Put the sugar, lemon zest and ginger pieces in a food processor and process 2-3 minutes until the zest and ginger are finely ground. Add the butter and process until creamed and smooth. Add the eggs. Process, scrape the bowl, and process some more until smooth. Scrape contents into a large bowl. Fold in dry ingredients along with the buttermilk or yogurt. Bake in prepared muffin pans at 400° F. for 20-25 minutes. Makes 12 muffins.

"This recipe is a favorite of our guests. It originated from Deborah Laurion, the first Thompson House chef. Deborah is no longer here, but we do still serve her recipes."
Marvin Bonta – Thompson House Inn

Stapleton Spurr

S tapleton Spurr is a European-style country bed and breakfast located four miles west of Aspen, five miles from Snowmass Village and two miles from the Aspen Airport. Excellent cross-country skiing trails are nearby. Cyclists use a paved bike path that is within 200 yards of the inn.

Guests sit by the fireplace in the Mediterranean-style living room or enjoy the lovely view of Mt. Daly, Aspen and Buttermilk Mountains from the deck.

INNKEEPERS: *Sam & Elizabeth Stapleton*
ADDRESS: *1370 Owl Creek Road; PO Box 98*
Aspen, CO 81612
TELEPHONE: *(970) 925-7322*
ROOMS: *4 Rooms; Shared baths*
OPEN: *Year-round*
CHILDREN: *Welcome*
ANIMALS: *Prohibited; Resident cats and dogs*
SMOKING: *Prohibited*

Bran Muffins

1 c. flour
1 c. Natural Health Bran, or bran of choice
1 t. baking soda
1/3 c. sugar
1 t. baking powder
6 T. oil
1 egg
3/4 c. chopped dates
1 c. boiling water

In a large bowl, mix flour, bran, baking soda, sugar and baking powder. In a separate bowl, combine oil, egg, dates and water. Add to bran mixture. Stir until combined. Bake at 400° F. for about 20-25 minutes. Makes 12 muffins.

Carol's Corner
Bran can usually be found in the bulk foods department of a grocery store. I used wheat bran when I tried this recipe and the results were perfect. The dates are a nice addition to these moist muffins.

St. Mary's Glacier

S t. Mary's Glacier Bed and Breakfast, at 10,500 feet, is the highest
B&B in North America. It borders Arapahoe National Forest and the
historic silver and gold rush trails. Guests enjoy such activities as hiking,
mountain biking, cross-country and world-class, downhill skiing.

Surrounded by snow-capped Continental Divide peaks, a cascading
waterfall and crystalline high mountain lakes, the inn is just a short hike
from the southernmost glacier in North America.

INNKEEPERS:	*Jackie & Steve Jacquin*
ADDRESS:	*336 Crest Drive*
	Idaho Springs, CO 80452
TELEPHONE:	*(303) 567-4084*
ROOMS:	*5 Suites; All private baths*
OPEN:	*Year-round*
CHILDREN:	*Not recommended*
ANIMALS:	*Prohibited*
SMOKING:	*Restricted to outdoor areas*

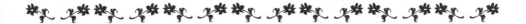

Southern Biscuit Muffins

Easy to make at the last minute!

2 1/2 c. flour
1/4 c. sugar
1 1/2 T. baking powder
3/4 c. cold butter or margarine
1 c. cold milk

Preheat oven to 400° F. Grease muffin pans. These muffins brown better on the sides and bottom when baked <u>without</u> paper liners.

In a large bowl, combine the flour, sugar and baking powder. Cut in butter until mixture resembles coarse crumbs. Stir in milk *just until mixture is moistened.* Spoon into muffin cups. Bake about 18-20 minutes or until golden. Remove from pan. Cool on wire rack. Makes 12 muffins.

> **Carol's Corner**
> *With a light, sweet taste, these are delicious! Soft and fluffy on the inside–light brown and crunchy on the outside.*

Elizabeth Street Guest House

Elizabeth Street Guest House is a beautifully restored American Four-square brick home, lovingly furnished with family antiques, plants, old quilts and handmade crafts. The leaded windows and oak woodwork are special features, as is the unique three-story miniature house in the entry hall.

Located in the historic heart of Fort Collins, Elizabeth Street Guest House is one block east of Colorado State University.

INNKEEPERS:	*John & Sheryl Clark*
ADDRESS:	*202 East Elizabeth Street*
	Ft. Collins, CO 80524
TELEPHONE:	*(970) 493-BEDS*
ROOMS:	*4 Rooms; Private and shared baths*
OPEN:	*Year-round*
CHILDREN:	*No restrictions*
ANIMALS:	*Prohibited; Resident dog*
SMOKING:	*Prohibited*

Raisin-Oatmeal Muffins

1 c. raisins
2 T. apple juice or water
3/4 c. flour
2 t. baking powder
3/4 t. salt
1/3 c. sugar
1 c. rolled oats
2 eggs
1/2 c. milk
1/4 c. vegetable oil

Topping
2 T. ground nuts
2 T. sugar
1 t. cinnamon

Prehcat oven to 400° F. Prepare muffin pans with vegetable oil spray or use liners.

Sprinkle raisins with apple juice (or water) and microwave for 30 seconds. Set aside to cool. In a large bowl, stir flour, baking powder, salt and sugar together thoroughly. Stir in oats and raisins (including juice). In a small bowl, combine eggs, milk and oil. Beat well with fork. Add wet ingredients to dry ingredients and stir just until moistened. Fill muffin cups about 2/3 full. Combine topping ingredients. Sprinkle onto muffins. Bake for 15-20 minutes or until top of muffins springs back when lightly touched. Makes 12 muffins.

BISCUITS
ROLLS
COFFEE CAKE
&
SCONES

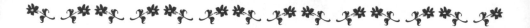

Barbara's

Barbara's Bed & Breakfast is nestled on Little Prospect Mountain in Estes Park. While sitting on the deck, guests enjoy beautiful scenery and perhaps catch a glimpse of the variety of wildlife.

A quaint antique and gift shop offers an assortment of old world treasures, crafts, and dried flower arrangements. Wedding packages that include a minister are available.

INNKEEPERS:	*Barbara Felte*
ADDRESS:	*255 Cyteworth; PO Box 540*
	Estes Park, CO 80517
TELEPHONE:	*(970) 586-5871; (800) 597-7903*
ROOMS:	*3 Rooms; 1 Suite; Shared and private baths*
OPEN:	*Year-round*
CHILDREN:	*Accepted on individual basis*
ANIMALS:	*Prohibited*
SMOKING:	*Smoking in the outdoors only*

Cinnamon Rolls

2 1/2 c. milk
2 pkgs. active dry yeast
1/3 c. sugar
1/3 c. oil
2 t. salt
3 t. baking powder
1 egg
6-7 c. flour
1/2 c. (1 stick) butter, melted

Filling Mixture
1/4 c. sugar
1 t. cinnamon
1/2 c. packed brown sugar

Scald milk; cool to lukewarm. Dissolve the 2 packages of yeast in 1/2 cup of the lukewarm milk. Add the yeast mixture, sugar, oil, salt, baking powder and egg to the rest of the milk. Mix well; then add flour until easy to handle. Knead until smooth. Place dough in a lightly oiled bowl. Cover and allow to rise until doubled in size. Punch down dough and roll into an 18x24-inch rectangle. Cover with the melted butter. Combine the filling ingredients and sprinkle on top of the butter. Roll the dough up tightly, jelly-roll fashion, starting with the 24-inch side; seal edges. Cut into 12 (2-inch) slices. At this point the slices can be frozen, then removed as needed, or placed in a greased pan, refrigerated and covered for up to 48 hours. If refrigerated, take rolls out and allow to rise, if needed. Bake at 350° F. until light brown, about 20 minutes. Let cool for about 10 minutes and then frost or drizzle with a vanilla glaze, using your favorite recipe. Makes 12.

The Mary Lawrence Inn

The Mary Lawrence Inn is nestled in the scenic Gunnison Valley between the San Juan and Elk Mountains. Originally built in 1885 by Nathan Weinberger, a local entrepreneur and saloon owner, its subsequent owner, Mary Axtell Lawrence, emigrated from Illinois to Colorado and finally settled in Gunnison in 1908. Mrs. Lawrence, a widow, served as a teacher and school administrator while operating her home as a boarding house.

This unique Bed and Breakfast was completely renovated in 1989.

INNKEEPERS:	*Pat & Jim Kennedy*
ADDRESS:	*601 North Taylor*
	Gunnison, CO 81230
TELEPHONE:	*(970) 641-3343*
ROOMS:	*4 Rooms; 1 Suite; All with private baths*
OPEN:	*Year-round*
CHILDREN:	*Ages six and older are welcome*
ANIMALS:	*Prohibited; Two resident cats*
SMOKING:	*Prohibited*

Flaky Cinnamon Rolls

Not enough time for yeast rolls? Make <u>these</u> in no time at all!

2 c. all-purpose flour
1 T. sugar
4 t. baking powder
1/2 t. salt
1/2 t. cream of tartar
1/2 c. shortening
3/4 c. milk

<u>Filling</u>
3 T. melted butter
1 c. brown sugar
1 t. cinnamon
1/2 c. pecans, finely chopped

Preheat oven to 400° F. Mix together the dry ingredients. Cut shortening into the dry mixture with a pastry blender, fork, or your fingertips until mixture resembles fine crumbs. Add milk to mixture and stir with fork ONLY until moistened. Put dough onto a floured board and knead gently about 10 times or until smooth. Roll into an 8x12-inch rectangle. Brush on melted butter. Combine brown sugar, cinnamon and nuts and sprinkle on evenly. Press topping into dough. Roll up dough, starting with long side, into a tight roll. Seal edges. Slice off 1-inch pieces and place cut side up on a baking sheet coated with cooking spray. Bake for 15 minutes or until golden. Makes 10-12 cinnamon rolls.

Back in Time

B uilt in 1903 by the proprietor of the Silver Shoe Clothing Company in Glenwood Springs, this charming Victorian Inn served as offices for local doctors and lawyers and as an antique store before becoming a modern bed and breakfast.

Fifteen years after browsing for antiques in that Victorian Inn, Ron and June Robinson restored and now operate it as the Back In Time Bed and Breakfast Inn.

INNKEEPERS:	*June & Ron Robinson*
ADDRESS:	*927 Cooper Avenue*
	Glenwood Springs, CO 81601
TELEPHONE:	*(970) 945-6183*
ROOMS:	*3 Rooms; All with private baths*
OPEN:	*Year-round*
CHILDREN:	*Children over 10 are welcome*
ANIMALS:	*Prohibited*
SMOKING:	*Prohibited*

Caramel Rolls

1 dozen frozen dough dinner rolls
1/3 c. brown sugar
1/3 c. butter
2 T. cream or evaporated milk
1/2 small pkg. (3.5 oz.) butterscotch pudding (not instant)
Nuts, as desired

Prepare a Bundt cake pan with cooking spray. Place rolls, side by side, in bottom of pan. Set aside. Melt butter in a saucepan. Add brown sugar and the cream or milk. Bring to a boil, cooking until all ingredients are one. Let cool before pouring over rolls. Then sprinkle 1/2 pkg. butterscotch pudding (use about 4 T. of dry mix and save other half for next time) and the nuts over the rolls. Cover the pan with waxed paper and leave on the counter overnight. Bake the next morning at 350° F. for 30-40 minutes. (Be sure to check after 30 minutes.) Immediately flip the pan over onto waxed paper or a serving plate. Makes 12 rolls.

Carol's Corner
What could lure family or friends to the breakfast table faster than these tempting, warm from the oven, caramel rolls? By using frozen bread dough, this is a quick and easy, make-ahead recipe.

Country Gardens

Country Gardens Bed and Breakfast was custom built in 1979. It is located on four acres with natural landscaping and great views of the Front Range of Colorado's Rocky Mountains.

The Doll Room contains dolls of all kinds, old and new. The Medallion Room features a medallion headboard bed with matching dresser and oval mirror. Roses are featured in the wallpaper, drapes and bed linens in the Rose Room.

INNKEEPERS:	*Arlie & Donna Munsie*
ADDRESS:	*1619 E. 136th Avenue; PO Box 33765*
	Northglenn, Co 80233
TELEPHONE:	*(303) 451-1724; (800) 475-1724*
ROOMS:	*4 Rooms; Private baths*
OPEN:	*Year-round*
CHILDREN:	*Children 12 and older are welcome*
ANIMALS:	*Prohibited*
SMOKING:	*Prohibited*

Refrigerated
Potato Rolls

Make-ahead! This dough can be refrigerated for several hours or up to one week. Be sure to allow time for the dough to rise when you actually make the rolls.

4 servings, instant mashed potatoes
5 c. flour, divided
1 pkg. active dry yeast
1 c. milk
1/2 c. shortening
1/2 c. sugar
1 t. salt
2 eggs

Prepare potatoes according to package directions. In a large bowl, stir together 2 cups of the flour and the package of yeast. In a saucepan, heat milk, shortening, sugar and salt over medium heat, just until warm. Stir in potatoes and add to the dry mixture. Add eggs and beat on low speed 1/2 minute. Scrape sides and beat 3 minutes on high speed. By hand, stir in remaining 3 cups flour to make a soft dough. (If dough is still too sticky to handle, stir in just a little more flour.) Place dough in a greased bowl, turn once, and cover. (The container should be large enough to allow the dough to expand some.) Refrigerate several hours or up to one week. To use, shape into rolls and put in a greased pan or muffin tins. Let rise until double in size, approximately 2 1/2 hours. Bake for 20-25 minutes at 350° F.

Carol's Corner
Served warm from the oven, these light and tender rolls will be the talk of your dinner table. Next time try Potato Cheese Rolls–when shaping the rolls, first knead in a little finely shredded cheddar cheese. Equally delicious!

The Kessey House

The Kessey Bed and Breakfast was part of the original site of the Spicer Lode discovered in 1891. The Kessey family has owned this grand Victorian for 60 of its 94 years, and they enjoy sharing its history and memories.

Mary and R.H. Atchison were the first owners. Little is known about them; however, Mary's ghost is believed to be present and lingers in the attic as a benevolent protector.

INNKEEPERS:	*Carol Kessey James*
ADDRESS:	*212 South Third Street*
	Victor, CO 80860
TELEPHONE:	*(719) 689-2235*
ROOMS:	*4 Rooms; Shared baths*
OPEN:	*Year-round*
CHILDREN:	*Welcome*
ANIMALS:	*Permitted*
SMOKING:	*Prohibited*

Golden Raisin Buns

1 c. water
1/2 c. butter
1 t. sugar
1 c. flour
1/4 t. salt
4 eggs
1/2 c. raisins

Combine water, butter and sugar in a pan. Bring to a boil. Add flour and salt all at once. Over low heat, beat with a wooden spoon for 1 minute or until mixture leaves sides of pan and forms a smooth thick dough. Remove from heat. Continue beating about 2 minutes to cool slightly. Add eggs one at a time, beating after each, until mixture has a satiny sheen. Stir in raisins. Drop dough from a tablespoon, about 2-inches apart, onto a greased baking sheet. Bake in preheated oven at 375° for 30-35 minutes, or until golden and firm. Frost while warm. Makes 24-30 small buns.

Frosting
1 T. butter
1 1/2 T. cream
1 c. powdered sugar
1/2 t. lemon juice
1/2 t. vanilla

Melt butter. Stir in cream. Remove from heat and stir in powdered sugar, lemon juice and vanilla. If needed, add more cream for spreading consistency.

"An Airedale was staying with his owner, a geologist, who was visiting the area. I was just getting ready to serve breakfast and had a tray of Golden Raisin Buns on the kitchen table. I heard something crash to the floor in the kitchen. The dog had pulled the whole tray off the table and was devouring all of the buns. I said to the geologist, 'Well, your dog just ate half of your breakfast. I hope you like pancakes!'"
Carol Kessey James – The Kessey House B&B

Plum House

P lum House Bed and Breakfast is located in Red Cliff one block from Shrine Pass. The owner, Sydney Summers, is an artist, gallery owner and gourmet cook. Sydney will prepare dinner with 24-hour notice. Breakfast includes her homemade muffins, rolls, and a variety of other delectable foods.

Guests enjoy the hot tub after a day of skiing or hiking or just lounge in the living room by the wood stove.

INNKEEPERS:	*Sydney Summers*
ADDRESS:	*236 Eagle Street; PO Box 41*
	Red Cliff, CO 81649
TELEPHONE:	*(970) 827-5881*
ROOMS:	*1 Room; Private bath*
OPEN:	*Year-round*
CHILDREN:	*Space prohibitive*
ANIMALS:	*Prohibited*
SMOKING:	*Prohibited*

Best Biscuits

Light and fluffy, these really are the best!

2 c. flour
4 t. baking powder
1/2 t. salt
1/2 t. cream of tartar
2 t. sugar
1/2 c. shortening (butter flavored Crisco is best)
2/3 c. milk

Sift together dry ingredients and cut in shortening until it resembles coarse crumbs. Mix in milk and stir only until dough is stiff. Turn out on a floured board and knead about 1/2 minute. Flatten to about 3/4-inch and cut with a glass dipped in flour. Place biscuits on an ungreased cookie sheet. Cook 10-13 minutes at 450° F.

"These are old-fashioned biscuits and wonderful with my homemade jams and jellies and preserves. Delicious!"
Sydney Summers – Plum House B&B

Posada de Sol y Sombra

Bed and Breakfast

The Posada de Sol y Sombra (Inn of Sun and Shadow) is sequestered behind a white picket fence on a quiet street in the southern Colorado town of LaVeta. This 1890's brick farmhouse is situated at the base of Cuchara Valley between the Sangre de Cristo mountain range and the lofty, skyscraping twin Spanish Peaks.

Paintings by local artists enhance the walls of this hospitable bed and breakfast inn.

INNKEEPERS:	*Betty & Carroll Elwell*
ADDRESS:	*PO Box 522*
	LaVeta, CO 81055
TELEPHONE:	*(719) 742-3159*
ROOMS:	*2 Rooms; Shared bath*
OPEN:	*Year-round*
CHILDREN:	*Welcome*
ANIMALS:	*Please call*
SMOKING:	*Prohibited*

Dried-Cherry Buttermilk Scones

2 c. all-purpose flour
1/3 c. sugar
1 1/2 t. baking powder
1/2 t. baking soda
6 T. butter, chilled
1/2 c. buttermilk
1 large egg
1 1/2 t. vanilla
2/3 c. dried sour cherries

Preheat oven to 400° F. In a large bowl, sift together the dry ingredients. Cut butter into 1/2-inch cubes and distribute over flour mixture. With a pastry blender, cut in the butter until the mixture resembles coarse crumbs. Stir together the buttermilk, egg and vanilla. Add to the flour mixture. Stir in the cherries. With lightly floured hands, pat the dough into an 8-inch diameter circle on an *ungreased* cookie sheet. With a serrated knife, cut into 8 separate wedges. Bake 18-20 minutes, or until a cake tester inserted into the center comes out clean. Cool for 5 minutes. Serve warm. Makes 8 scones.

"Scones have been so well-received they have become a notable part of our menus. Coming from Michigan, we like to use Michigan products such as Traverse City dried sour cherries."
Betty Elwell – Posada de Sol y Sombra

Castle Marne

Built in 1889, Castle Marne is considered by many to be the finest example of America's most eclectic architect, William Lang (designer of Unsinkable Molly Brown's house). Its history glows through the hand-rubbed woods, the renowned circular stained glass Peacock Window and original ornate fireplace.

"No one can truly own any part of the heritage of a city and its people. That's why we consider ourselves as merely caretakers of the Castle Marne, and it's a privilege we cherish."

~ Owners, Castle Marne

INNKEEPERS:	*Jim & Diane Peiker; Louis & Melissa Feher-Peiker*
ADDRESS:	*1572 Race Street*
	Denver, CO 80206
TELEPHONE:	*(303) 331-0621; (800) 92-MARNE*
ROOMS:	*8 Rooms; 1 Suite; All with private baths*
OPEN:	*Year-round*
CHILDREN:	*Not suitable for children under 10*
ANIMALS:	*Prohibited*
SMOKING:	*Prohibited*

The Queen's Royal Scones

3/4 c. currants soaked in liqueur of choice (we use sherry)
3 1/4 c. all-purpose flour
3/4 c. sugar
2 1/2 t. baking powder
1/2 t. baking soda
3/4 c. firm butter, cut into small pieces
1 c. buttermilk

Soak currants in liqueur for at least 2 hours. In a large bowl, stir together the flour, sugar, baking powder and baking soda until thoroughly blended. Using a pastry cutter, cut the butter into the flour mixture until it resembles cornmeal. Stir in the <u>drained</u> currants. Make a well in the center of the flour mixture and add the buttermilk all at once. Stir with a fork until the batter pulls away from the side of the bowl. Gather the dough together with your hands into a ball. Put on a lightly floured board and pat into a circle about 3/4-inch high. Handle the dough as little as possible. Using a small heart or daisy shaped cookie cutter, cut into individual scones. Place 1 1/2-inches apart on a lightly greased cookie sheet. Bake in a 425° F. oven for 12 minutes, or until the tops are lightly browned. Serve warm with creme fraiche and raspberry jam or honey butter.

*"We have tasted scones from many tearooms and truly
believe this is the finest recipe we have tasted or made
for our teas and Victorian luncheons."*
Diane Peiker – Castle Marne

Eastholme in the Rockies

D esignated a Ute Pass landmark by the 1976 Bicentennial Committee, Eastholme is the oldest of a group of resort hotels that once flourished between scenic Manitou Springs and Cripple Creek. Authentically restored and furnished with antiques, Eastholme was the sole recipient of Colorado's Historical Preservation Award for 1989.

Notable guests have included Dwight and Mamie Eisenhower, a European monarch and most recently a lady "ghost."

INNKEEPERS:	*Terry Thompson and family*
ADDRESS:	*4445 Haggerman; PO Box 98*
	Cascade, CO 80809
TELEPHONE:	*(719) 684-9901*
ROOMS:	*4 Rooms; 2 Suites; Shared and private baths*
OPEN:	*Year-round*
CHILDREN:	*Welcome*
ANIMALS:	*Guest pets permitted on individual basis*
SMOKING:	*Prohibited*

Scones

5 c. flour
2 T. baking powder
1 c. sugar
1 c. (2 sticks) butter, cut up
Buttermilk, as needed

Mix the flour, baking powder and sugar in a food processor with the steel blade. Add the butter a little at a time until you have the consistency of cornmeal. *At this point, you can put it in a zip lock bag in the refrigerator and keep it for at least a month.* Take as much of the mixture as you think you will need, and add buttermilk slowly, a little at a time until you get a ball of dough, not too soft. If you get it too soft, just add more of the flour mixture. On a lightly floured board, knead the dough slightly and pat flat until it is about 1/2-inch thick. Cut with a sharp biscuit cutter and place on an ungreased cookie sheet. Bake for 12-15 minutes at 350° F. until *slightly* brown. Serve with jam. Makes about 30 scones.

Carol's Corner
Using a food processor is a fast and easy way to prepare this "do-ahead" scone mix. You can have warm, tasty scones on the breakfast table in no time at all.

The Robin's Nest

THE ROBIN'S NEST
BED & BREAKFAST

Located on 2 1/3 acres in Bighorn Sheep Canyon, Robin's Nest Bed and Breakfast overlooks the Arkansas Valley. From the wrap-around deck, guests enjoy a fantastic view of the mountains.

Sports enthusiasts enjoy rafting, Jeep rides, horseback riding, golfing, fishing, hiking, rockhounding or leisurely walks in the mountains through high meadows or along rushing streams.

INNKEEPERS:	*Mary McConathy*
ADDRESS:	*9134 Highway 50*
	Howard, CO 81233
TELEPHONE:	*(719) 942-4176*
ROOMS:	*4 Rooms; 1 Suite; All with private baths*
OPEN:	*Year-round*
CHILDREN:	*Welcome*
ANIMALS:	*Prohibited*
SMOKING:	*No smoking in the house*

Hildegarde's
Sour Cream Coffee Cake

1 c. (2 sticks) margarine, softened
1 1/4 c. sugar
2 eggs
1 c. sour cream
1 t. vanilla
2 c. flour
1/2 t. baking soda
1 1/2 t. baking powder

<u>Topping</u>
3 T. sugar
1 1/2 t. cinnamon
3/4 c. nuts, chopped

DO NOT PREHEAT OVEN. Cream together the margarine, sugar and eggs. Blend in the sour cream and vanilla. Sift the dry ingredients together and add to the creamed mixture. Put 1/2 of the batter into a greased and floured angel food cake pan or Bundt pan. Combine topping ingredients. Sprinkle 1/2 of the topping onto the batter in the pan. Add remaining batter and sprinkle on the rest of the topping. Bake at 350° F. for approximately 55 minutes. Do not overbake. Cake is done when toothpick inserted in cake comes out clean.

"This recipe is large and can serve up to 12 people. I often cut it in half and freeze part for later use. My Aunt Hildegarde traveled all over the world with her minister husband and baked and served this coffee cake, which was a hit everywhere."
Mary McConathy – Robin's Nest

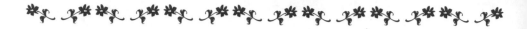

Alpen Rose

Hidden away just minutes from downtown Winter Park, the Alpen Rose Bed and Breakfast boasts of "Austrian warmth and hospitality." A large deck off the lodge's common room affords a panoramic view highlighted by the backside of the majestic Front Range.

During the summer months, the owners entrust management of the Alpen Rose to friends and travel to Germany. There they run a hiking lodge called Storhaus in Berchtesgaden.

INNKEEPERS:	*Robin & Rupert Sommerauer*
ADDRESS:	*244 Forest Trail; PO Box 769*
	Winter Park, CO 80482
TELEPHONE:	*(970) 726-5039; (800) 531-1373*
ROOMS:	*4 Rooms; 1 Suite; All with private baths*
OPEN:	*Mid-November through Mid-September*
CHILDREN:	*Accepted*
ANIMALS:	*Prohibited*
SMOKING:	*Prohibited*

Austrian Apple Strudel

1 sheet frozen prepared puff pastry
  (Pepperidge Farm recommended)
1 large green apple (Granny Smith)
2-3 T. butter
1/3-1/2 c. golden raisins
8-10 dried apricot halves, cut in quarters
1/4 c. water
1/4 c. packed light brown sugar
1/2 t. ground cinnamon
1/4 t. ground nutmeg
1 egg yolk beaten with 1 T. water

Thaw puff pastry. Cut and core apple and chop into small pieces, 1/2-inch size. Over medium heat, melt butter in a large skillet. Add apple, raisins and apricots. Mix well and sauté a few minutes. Add water, brown sugar, cinnamon and nutmeg. Cover and simmer for about 10 minutes. Cool. Place pastry on a flat surface and distribute apple mixture down the middle of pastry sheet. Make 2 1/2-inch long cuts diagonally along both sides of exposed pastry at 1 1/2-inch intervals. Fold strips over apples alternating from left to right. Press dough together where ends overlap. With fork tines, seal top and bottom edge of dough. *At this point, refrigerate for 30 minutes or wrap and freeze for later use.* At time of baking, place strudel on a cookie sheet covered with parchment paper, or use an insulated cookie sheet, to prevent overbrowning on the bottom of the pastry. Brush with egg wash. Bake in a preheated oven at 425° F. for 25 minutes or until strudel is light golden. Serves 4-6.

"I like to prepare the strudel in advance and freeze until baking time. It's a favorite at the breakfast table and is also wonderful in the afternoon with tea or coffee."
Robin Sommerauer – Alpen Rose B&B

PANCAKES
WAFFLES
&
CREPES

Valley View

Valley View was meticulously hand-crafted by its owners to insure the proper blend between modern amenities and old-fashioned quality and comfort. It is a live-in museum with artifacts, antiques and art work that were collected throughout Europe and North America.

The owners happily board horses for the Western enthusiasts who want to explore or hunt the vast reaches of the Grand Mesa, the world's largest flattop mountain.

INNKEEPERS:	*Lou & Jan Purin*
ADDRESS:	*888 21 Road*
	Fruita, CO 81521
TELEPHONE:	*(970) 858-9503*
ROOMS:	*3 Rooms; Private and shared baths*
OPEN:	*Year-round*
CHILDREN:	*Children over the age of 10 are welcome*
ANIMALS:	*Dogs permitted outside; Can board horses*
SMOKING:	*Not allowed indoors*

Apple Pecan Pancakes

1 c. all-purpose flour
2 T. brown sugar
2 t. baking powder
1/2 t. salt
1/2 t. ground cinnamon
3/4 c. plus 2 T. milk
2 eggs, separated
1 t. vanilla extract
1/2 c. peeled and finely chopped apple
1/2 c. finely chopped pecans
Apple Spice Syrup (recipe below)

In a bowl, combine flour, brown sugar, baking powder, salt and cinnamon. Stir in milk, egg yolks and vanilla. Add apple and pecans. Beat egg whites until stiff peaks form, then fold into batter. Using a 1/4 cup measure, pour batter onto a hot, greased griddle or skillet. Turn when bubbles begin to form and the edges are golden. Cook until the second side is golden. Makes 12 pancakes. Serve with Apple Spice Syrup.

Apple Spice Syrup
1/4 c. packed brown sugar
2 T. cornstarch
1/4 t. ground allspice
1/8 t. ground nutmeg
1 3/4 c. apple juice or cider

In a saucepan, combine brown sugar, cornstarch, allspice and nutmeg. Mix well. Add juice or cider. Cook and stir over medium heat until syrup is bubbly and slightly thickened. Makes 1 3/4 cups.

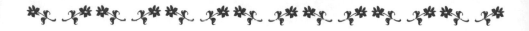

Back in Time

Built in 1903 by the proprietor of the Silver Shoe Clothing Company in Glenwood Springs, this charming Victorian Inn served as offices for local doctors and lawyers and as an antique store before becoming a modern bed and breakfast.

Fifteen years after browsing for antiques in that Victorian Inn, Ron and June Robinson restored and now operate it as the Back In Time Bed and Breakfast Inn.

INNKEEPERS:	*June & Ron Robinson*
ADDRESS:	*927 Cooper Avenue*
	Glenwood Springs, CO 81601
TELEPHONE:	*(970) 945-6183*
ROOMS:	*3 Rooms; All with private baths*
OPEN:	*Year-round*
CHILDREN:	*Children over 10 are welcome*
ANIMALS:	*Prohibited*
SMOKING:	*Prohibited*

High Rise
Apple Pancakes

Filling
1/4 c. margarine
4-6 c. peeled and sliced apples
1/4 c. sugar
1/2 t. cinnamon

Melt margarine in a skillet. Add apples, sugar and cinnamon. Cook until apples are soft. Set aside.

Batter
2 eggs, beaten
1/2 c. flour
1/2 c. milk
1/4 t. salt

Beat batter ingredients together until smooth. Heat an ovenproof 8-inch or 10-inch skillet in a 450° F. oven until very hot. Remove from oven and add 1 tablespoon margarine; immediately pour in the batter. Bake on bottom rack for 10 minutes. It will puff up. Remove from the oven and fill with the apples. Top with preserves or maple syrup, if you wish. Serve from the skillet at the table. Cut into pie-shaped pieces. Serves 4-6.

Carol's Corner
The filling by itself is delicious and can be used in a variety of ways. Use it as a side dish to serve with ham, turkey or pork. Or offer it as a dessert topped with whipped cream or a scoop of vanilla ice cream.

Black Dog Inn

Built in 1910, the Black Dog Inn was one of the earliest homes built in Estes Park. Snuggled among towering pine and aspen on a rolling acre, it affords an expansive view of Lumpy Ridge and the Estes Valley. A footpath that runs in front of the inn leads to nearby attractions.

The innkeepers, having experience in hiking, skiing and snowshoeing, happily share books, maps and back country knowledge with their guests.

INNKEEPERS: *Pete & Jane Princehorn*
ADDRESS: *650 S. St. Vrain Avenue; PO Box 4659*
Estes Park, CO 80517
TELEPHONE: *(970) 586-0374*
ROOMS: *4 Rooms; All with private baths*
OPEN: *Year-round*
CHILDREN: *Welcome over the age of 12*
ANIMALS: *Prohibited; Resident dog*
SMOKING: *Prohibited*

Pumpkin Granola Pancakes

2 c. biscuit mix
2 T. packed brown sugar
2 t. ground cinnamon
1 t. ground allspice
1 (12 oz.) can evaporated milk
1/2 c. canned pumpkin
2 T. vegetable oil
2 eggs
1 t. vanilla extract
Granola (one with raisins is especially good)

Combine biscuit mix, brown sugar, cinnamon and allspice. Add evaporated milk, pumpkin, oil, eggs and vanilla. Beat until smooth. Using a 1/4 cup measure, pour batter onto hot, oiled griddle or skillet. Sprinkle some granola on top of batter. Cook until bubbly on top. Turn and cook until done. Remove from griddle and keep warm in oven. Serve with maple syrup and hot apple sauce. Makes 12-16 pancakes.

Double Diamond

WILDERNESS GUIDE SERVICE

The Double Diamond Ranch overlooks Ruedi Reservoir in the upper Frying Pan River Valley. It lies in the heart of the Rocky Mountain area that encompasses the Hunter-Frying Pan Wilderness, a pristine region, accessible only by foot or horseback.

"This area possesses the isolation, climate and spectacular scenery that wilderness represents, and our guests leave with memories of a western adventure."

~ Owner, Joan Wheeler

INNKEEPERS:	*Joan Wheeler*
ADDRESS:	*PO Box 2*
	Meredith, CO 81642
TELEPHONE:	*(970) 927-3404*
ROOMS:	*2 Rooms; Private baths*
OPEN:	*Year-round*
CHILDREN:	*Children welcome*
ANIMALS:	*Permitted if well-behaved*
SMOKING:	*Prohibited*

Gingerbread Pancakes with Nectarine Cream Sauce

1 1/3 c. flour
1 t. baking powder
1/4 t. salt
1/4 t. baking soda
1/2 t. ground ginger
1 t. cinnamon
1 egg
1 1/4 c. milk
1/4 c. molasses
3 T. oil
Nectarine Cream Sauce (recipe below)

Combine flour, baking powder, salt, baking soda, ginger and cinnamon. In a large bowl, beat egg with milk. Beat in molasses and then oil. Add flour mixture and stir until just combined. Batter will be slightly lumpy. Cook on a hot, greased griddle or skillet until puffed, bubbled and dry around edges. Turn and brown on other side. Makes 8 good-sized pancakes. Serves 3-4. Serve with Nectarine Cream Sauce.

Nectarine Cream Sauce
1/2 c. sugar
1/2 c. light corn syrup
1/2 c. whipping cream
1 t. vanilla
1 nectarine, diced

Combine sugar, corn syrup and whipping cream in a 1 quart pan. Cook, stirring constantly, until sugar is dissolved. Simmer 2 minutes or until slightly thickened. Remove from heat. Stir in vanilla and nectarine. Makes approximately 2 cups.

Lost Canyon Lake Lodge

Bed and Breakfast

L ost Canyon Lake Lodge is a contemporary, two-story log home nestled in the pines overlooking Lost Canyon Lake Reservoir. Guests climb above the treeline at 12,000 feet, explore the archaeological ruins of the Anasazi Civilization or descend into the depths of the sheer redrock canyon walls.

With 321 days of sunshine, the Cortez-Dolores-Mancos area encompasses some of the most diverse and beautiful country in Colorado.

INNKEEPERS:	*Beth Newman & Ken Nickson*
ADDRESS:	*PO Box 1289*
	Dolores, CO 81323
TELEPHONE:	*(970) 882-4913; (800) 992-1098*
ROOMS:	*4 Rooms; Private baths*
OPEN:	*Year-round*
CHILDREN:	*Welcome*
ANIMALS:	*Prohibited*
SMOKING:	*Permitted outside only*

Blueberry Upside-Down Pancake

2 T. margarine
1 can (16 1/2 oz.) Oregon blueberries
1 c. baking mix (preferably Bisquick)
1 egg
1/2 c. milk

Melt margarine in 9-inch pie plate. Swirl plate to spread margarine evenly. Drain blueberries. Put berries into pie plate and spread evenly over bottom. Prepare batter by combining the baking mix, egg and milk. Stir with a spoon, just until moistened. Pour batter over blueberries. Bake in 400° F. oven for approximately 20 minutes, or until golden brown. Serves 4. Serve with blueberry and maple syrups. Experiment with other berries and flavored syrups.

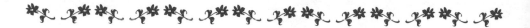

The Manor

The Manor was built in 1890 during Ouray's mining boom. This meticulously restored Georgian Victorian hybrid (National Historic Register) is the recipient of *The Historical Society's Preservation Award* for "noteworthy restoration of a historical building".

Known as the *Switzerland of America*, the high peaks and wilderness that surround The Manor make for a majestic setting.

INNKEEPERS:	*Joel & Diane Kramer*
ADDRESS:	*317 Second Street; PO Box 745*
	Ouray, CO 81427
TELEPHONE:	*(970) 325-4574*
ROOMS:	*7 Rooms; All with private baths*
OPEN:	*Year-round*
CHILDREN:	*No small children*
ANIMALS:	*Prohibited*
SMOKING:	*Prohibited*

Fresh Ginger Pancakes with Rhubarb, Pineapple, Strawberry Sauce

2 eggs
3 c. all-purpose flour
1 t. salt
2 t. baking soda
6 T. butter, melted and cooled
3 c. buttermilk
1/2 c. milk
3 T. fresh ginger, peeled and grated (food processor is easiest way)
Rhubarb, Pineapple, Strawberry Sauce (recipe below)

In a large bowl, beat eggs. Add the rest of the ingredients and mix until smooth. Using a 1/4 cup measure, pour batter onto a hot, greased griddle or skillet. When top side bubbles, turn and cook other side until golden brown. It's important to flip pancakes only once to avoid a rough, leathery texture. Sprinkle with powdered sugar. Garnish with cantaloupe, kiwi, and strawberries for an attractive array of colors. Serve Rhubarb, Pineapple, Strawberry Sauce in a separate dish. Makes 10-12 pancakes. Serves 5-6.

Rhubarb, Pineapple, Strawberry Sauce
3 c. rhubarb (fresh or frozen), chopped
1 c. sugar
1 (8 oz.) can crushed pineapple, drained
1 c. strawberries (fresh or frozen), diced

In a saucepan over medium heat, cook the rhubarb and sugar for about 15 minutes until tender. Stir frequently until it has a soft sauce consistency. Then add the pineapple and strawberries. Stir over low heat for a few minutes until warm.

Steamboat Valley Guest House

Guests of the Steamboat Valley Bed and Breakfast enjoy a nourishing, homemade breakfast of Swedish pancakes, green chili cheese soufflé or a steaming bowl of Irish oatmeal before a day on the slopes or a hike in the Rockies. Later they relax by the wildflower garden.

Business travelers are welcome. As one guest said, "Thanks for making my business trip not feel like business".

INNKEEPERS:	*Alice & George Lund*
ADDRESS:	*1245 Crawford Avenue; PO Box 773815*
	Steamboat Springs, Co 80477
TELEPHONE:	*(970) 870-9017; (800) 530-3866*
ROOMS:	*3 Rooms; 1 Suite; All with private baths*
OPEN:	*Year-round*
CHILDREN:	*Accommodations not suitable for*
	young children
ANIMALS:	*Prohibited*
SMOKING:	*Prohibited*

Swedish Pancakes

6 eggs
1/4 c. sugar
1/2 c. butter, melted
3/4 t. salt
2 1/4 c. flour
5 c. milk
1/2 c. lingonberries
Sour cream

Separate eggs. Place whites in small bowl, cover, and refrigerate. Place egg yolks in large mixing bowl and beat with sugar until light. Blend in butter and salt. Gradually add flour alternately with milk and beat until smooth. Cover and refrigerate a few hours or overnight. To cook, oil hot griddle lightly. Beat egg whites to soft peaks and carefully fold into batter. Use dipper to make small cakes and brown lightly on both sides. Serve immediately in small stacks on heated plates. Top each serving with 1 tablespoon lingonberries and a dollop of sour cream. Serves 6-8.

Carol's Corner
These pancakes are very thin and delicate, almost like a crepe. Doreen's husband Don is of Swedish descent and is very fond of Swedish pancakes. His mother rolls the pancakes with a Lingonberry sauce inside. The above recipe will work for rolled pancakes. Fill with any fruit filling of your choice.

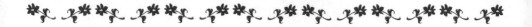

Plum House

Located one block from Shrine Pass, Plum House Bed and Breakfast is the plum-colored house on Eagle street in Red Cliff. The owner, Sydney Summers, is an artist, gallery owner and gourmet cook. With 24-hour notice, Sydney will prepare a special dinner for guests.

One bedroom is available, featuring a king-sized bed with electric blanket and down comforter and pillows.

INNKEEPERS: *Sydney Summers*
ADDRESS: *236 Eagle Street; PO Box 41*
Red Cliff, CO 81649
TELEPHONE: *(970) 827-5881*
ROOMS: *1 Room; Private bath*
OPEN: *Year-round*
CHILDREN: *Space prohibitive*
ANIMALS: *Prohibited*
SMOKING: *Prohibited*

Clafouti

1 lb. fresh plums, cut in quarters
1/4 c. sugar
2 eggs
1/2 c. milk
3 t. sour cream or plain yogurt
1/2 t. vanilla
1/2 c. flour
Dash salt
1 T. butter, approximately

"In the late summer or early fall, when the dark-skinned, golden interiored Italian prune-plums come in, this is a great dish, and is served instead of fruit with breakfast."
Sydney Summers – Plum House B&B

Toss plums with sugar. Set aside. Mix eggs, milk, sour cream, vanilla, flour and salt. Whisk well. Put the butter into a 9-inch pie plate and place in oven at 375° F. Let butter melt and begin to sizzle. Pour enough batter into plate to coat bottom and return to oven until set – about 2 or 3 minutes. Place plums, along with their juices, into plate and pour the rest of the uncooked batter over it. Bake for about 35-40 minutes longer. Cut as you would a piece of pie and serve hot. Tastes great cold, too!

Carol's Corner
Clafouti originated in France. There are many variations, but they all basically consist of a pancake-like batter and fruit. This recipe also makes a great dessert. Sprinkle about 2 teaspoons sugar over the top of the Clafouti the last 10 minutes of baking. Let cool on a wire rack about 5-10 minutes. It will fall a bit as it cools. Cut into wedges and top with whipped cream.

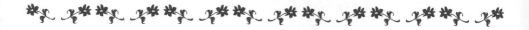

The Lovelander

T he Lovelander is a rambling Victorian built in 1902, just as Loveland's thriving sugar beet industry produced a bustling downtown economy. Originally a private home, the inn was a residence for teachers, an office for a country doctor and a boarding house.

Seasonally, guests enjoy film and craft festivals, including the largest outdoor sculpture show and sale in the nation, "Sculpture in the Park".

INNKEEPERS: *Bob & Marilyn Wiltgen*
ADDRESS: *217 West 4th Street*
Loveland, CO 80537
TELEPHONE: *(970) 669-0798; (800) 459-6694*
ROOMS: *11 Rooms; All with private baths*
CHILDREN: *Children welcome over the age of 10*
ANIMALS: *Prohibited*
SMOKING: *Prohibited*

Pumpkin Apple Waffles with Caramel Pecan Sauce

1/2 c. canned pumpkin
1 1/2 c. milk
3 eggs, beaten
1 c. flour
2 t. baking powder
2 T. sugar
1/2 t. salt
1/2 t. nutmeg
1/4 t. ground ginger
2 c. chopped, unpeeled apple, divided
Caramel Pecan Sauce (recipe below)

Combine pumpkin, milk and eggs. Add sifted dry ingredients to pumpkin mixture, stirring just until mixture is combined. Stir in 1 cup chopped apple. The batter can be stored in the refrigerator overnight. Cook on a preheated waffle iron that has been oiled or sprayed with food release spray. (Cooked waffles can be laid directly on the rack, uncovered, and held in a 200° oven.) To serve, dust prewarmed plates with powdered sugar. Sprinkle a few pinches of ground cinnamon around the edge of the plate. Center 2 waffles on the plate and top with some reserved chopped apple. Drizzle with Caramel Pecan Sauce.

Caramel Pecan Sauce
1 c. unsalted butter
2 1/2 c. brown sugar
1/4 t. salt
1/4 c. light corn syrup
1 c. heavy whipping cream
1 1/2 c. chopped toasted pecans

Melt butter in a saucepan over low heat. Add brown sugar and salt. Cook on low until melted and smooth. Stir in syrup. Cook on low 5-10 minutes. Stir in cream and cook for 5 more minutes. (Cook very slowly or sauce will turn sugary.) Stir in pecans. Sauce can be made ahead and refrigerated or frozen. Warm before serving. It can be thinned with half & half or cream for a milkier sauce.

Gunbarrel Guest House

Q uiet and warmly elegant, the Gunbarrel Guest House features
lodging in the European style while offering all the amenities of a
large hotel. Full-service conference and meeting rooms, ideal for
weekend retreats, seminars and all types of meetings can be easily
arranged.

The great room and patio provide a lovely atmosphere for special events
such as weddings, rehearsal dinners and corporate cocktail parties. They
also host murder mysteries!

INNKEEPERS:	*Carolann Evans*
ADDRESS:	*6901 Lookout Road*
	Boulder, CO 80301
TELEPHONE:	*(303) 530-1513*
ROOMS:	*13 Rooms; All with private baths*
OPEN:	*Year-round*
CHILDREN:	*Welcome*
ANIMALS:	*Please call before bringing animals*
SMOKING:	*Prohibited*

Whole Wheat Buttermilk Waffles

3/4 c. whole wheat flour
3/4 c. all-purpose flour
2 t. baking powder
3/4 t. baking soda
1/2 t. salt
2 T. sugar
3 eggs
1 1/2 c. buttermilk
3/4 c. (1 1/2 sticks) butter, melted
1/4 c. milk, if needed

Put the flours into a small mixing bowl. Add the baking powder, baking soda, salt, and sugar. Stir with a fork to blend. In a large mixing bowl, beat eggs and combine with buttermilk and butter. Add dry ingredients to wet ingredients and stir just until combined. If batter is too thick, add a small amount of milk. Cook on hot waffle iron according to manufacturer's directions.

"As we are primarily an Inn that caters to the corporate traveler, we have a lot of repeat guests. One of our regulars once mentioned that it would be nice to incorporate something a bit different into our standard continental-plus style breakfast. He suggested occasionally offering waffles. (Most of our guests prefer low-fat, healthy breakfasts, like bagels, cereal, etc.) We decided to start 'Waffle Wednesdays'...and it has become so much fun, and so popular with the guests, that I think some of them even plan their business trips so they can be here for it! We always use the above recipe and offer several toppings (blueberries, peaches, bananas, walnuts, etc.) It's been several years of doing this now, and that same guest still stays here. Even when we're full, those that have to stay at a different hotel will come for waffles – and we never charge them!"
Carolann Evans – Gunbarrel Guest House

Wildridge Inn

T he Wildridge Inn is a beautiful, Southwestern adobe villa situated
high on a ridge of sage and wildflowers just minutes from Vail and
Beaver Creek. This romantic, serene hideaway offers its guests breathtaking views of the majestic Colorado Rockies.

The antique accents, Indian pottery and rugs all add to the warm,
wonderful ambiance of this tastefully decorated inn, located near skiing,
hiking, golf, restaurants and shopping.

INNKEEPERS:	*S. Kristin Goddard*
ADDRESS:	*PO Box 2123*
	Avon, CO 81620
TELEPHONE:	*(970) 949-4459*
ROOMS:	*2 Rooms; 1 Suite; Private and shared baths*
OPEN:	*Year-round*
CHILDREN:	*Children over the age of 12 are welcome*
ANIMALS:	*Prohibited; Resident dog*
SMOKING:	*Limited to outside patios*

Raised Waffles

1/2 c. warm water
1 pkg. dry yeast
2 c. warm milk
1/2 c. butter or margarine, melted
1 t. salt
1 t. sugar
2 c. flour
2 eggs
1/4 t. baking soda

Pour warm water into a large mixing bowl. Add yeast to water and let stand for 5 minutes to dissolve. Add warm milk, melted butter, salt, sugar and flour to yeast mixture and beat with mixer until blended and smooth. Cover bowl with plastic wrap and let stand overnight at room temperature. The mixture will grow. Just before cooking waffles, beat in eggs and baking soda. Stir until well mixed. Batter will be thin. Pour batter onto hot waffle iron and bake until done. Makes 6-8 waffles.

Tip: Leftover batter can be refrigeratcd and kept for several days.

Shenandoah Inn

T he Shenandoah Inn Bed and Breakfast is a recently restored home on two private riverfront acres on the Gold Medal trout waters of the Frying Pan River. Within walking distance of the restaurants and shops of Basalt, it is centrally located 20 minutes from Aspen and 25 minutes from the Glenwood hot springs pool.

With 20 years of professional cooking experience, Bob Ziets, the owner, treats guests to full gourmet breakfasts.

INNKEEPERS:	*Bob & Terri Ziets*
ADDRESS:	*0600 Frying Pan Road; PO Box 578*
	Basalt, CO 81621
TELEPHONE:	*(970) 927-4991*
ROOMS:	*2 Rooms; 1 Suite; 1 Cabin that sleeps six*
OPEN:	*Year-round*
CHILDREN:	*Well-behaved children over 12 are welcome*
ANIMALS:	*Prohibited*
SMOKING:	*Prohibited*

Shenandoah
Apple Walnut Crepes

Batter
3 eggs
3/4 c. milk
1/4 t. salt
3/4 c. flour
1/3 c. water

"A special recipe that celebrates the year-round apple. Not for the faint-of-heart!"
Terri & Bob Ziets – Shenandoah Inn

Whisk batter ingredients until smooth. Lightly spray 8-inch skillet with cooking spray and when hot, pour in small amount of batter, just enough to thinly coat bottom of skillet. Cook both sides over medium-high heat, until golden brown. Gently remove from pan; place on cloth towel to cool slightly. Prepare the rest of the crepes. Makes 12 crepes. Serves 6.

Filling
6 Granny Smith apples, peeled and sliced semi-thin
2 T. lemon juice
1/3 c. raisins
1/2 c. chopped walnuts
3 T. brown sugar
3 t. cinnamon
Pinch cloves
6 T. butter
1/3 c. light cream
1/2 c. dark rum or apple juice
Whipped cream, finely chopped nuts, powdered sugar, for garnish

Toss apple slices with lemon juice. Add raisins, walnuts, brown sugar, cinnamon and cloves. Heat butter in large pan. Sauté apple mixture on medium heat for 2 minutes, stirring constantly. Add cream and rum (or apple juice). Continue cooking for another minute or two until bubbling. Do not overcook – apples should stay firm. Arrange crepes on 6 warm plates, 2 per plate. Using a slotted spoon, fill with apple filling and a dollop of whipped cream. Fold tops in toward center. Drizzle folded crepes with syrup from pan, and dust with finely chopped nuts and powdered sugar.

Engelmann Pines

From its Rocky Mountain perch, this spacious modern lodge offers spectacular views of the Continental Divide. A free bus ferries skiers from the front door to some of Colorado's best ski slopes. Cross-country ski aficionados will find a trail just across the road.

When the snow melts, guests enjoy golfing, hiking, fishing and horseback riding. In the mornings, eager sports enthusiasts fill up on marzipan cake, muesli and fresh fruit crepes.

INNKEEPERS:	*Heinz & Margaret Engel*
ADDRESS:	*PO Box 1305*
	Winter Park, CO 80482
TELEPHONE:	*(970) 726-4632; (800) 992-9512*
ROOMS:	*7 Rooms; Private and shared baths*
OPEN:	*Year-round*
CHILDREN:	*Welcome*
ANIMALS:	*Prohibited*
SMOKING:	*Prohibited*

Crab Crepes

Crab Mixture
2 T. butter
2 T. flour
1 c. milk
1 (8 oz.) pkg. cream cheese
1 lb. crab meat, or imitation crab
2 T. ketchup
Szechuan seasoning, small amount to taste

Melt butter in heavy pan. Add flour and stir with a wire whisk, being careful not to burn mixture. Add milk and continue whisking until it begins to thicken. Add cream cheese and stir until melted. Add crab meat, ketchup and Szechuan seasoning. Set aside and make the crepes.

Crepe Batter
4 eggs
1/2 c. milk
1/2 c. water
2 T. melted butter
1 t. vanilla
2 t. sugar
1/2 t. salt
1 c. flour

Mix together all ingredients, except flour, with electric mixer until well blended. Add flour and continue to mix until all lumps are gone. Heat a 5-inch Ironstone skillet over medium heat. The batter will grease the pan, but you may need a few drops of oil to start. Add a small amount of batter and rotate the pan to spread the batter evenly. Brown gently on both sides. Fill crepes with warm crab mixture. Serves 8.

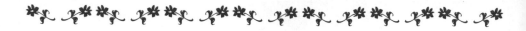

Annabelle's

A nnabelle's Bed and Breakfast, located in Summit County, provides the perfect place to sip espresso or herbal tea while gazing at snow-capped mountains. It is just a short distance from Arapahoe Basin, Copper Mountain, Breckenridge, Loveland and Vail ski resorts.

Before guests depart, they are asked to fill out an evaluation form rating the various aspects of the inn. One guest added a new category: Elmo, the dog. He was given 100 on a scale of 1 - 10.

INNKEEPERS:	*Tim & Ann Mealey*
ADDRESS:	*276 Snowberry Way*
	Dillon, CO 80435
TELEPHONE:	*(970) 468-8667*
ROOMS:	*3 Rooms; Two form a suite*
OPEN:	*Year-round*
CHILDREN:	*Children under 12 are FREE! (In their parent's room)*
ANIMALS:	*Prohibited*
SMOKING:	*Prohibited*

Cheese Blintzes

Crepe Batter
1 c. cold water
4 eggs
2 c. flour
1 c. cold milk
1/2 t. salt
4 T. melted butter

"This recipe looks complex and has lots of ingredients, but it's really quite easy. You can use low-fat products and the recipe is still terrific. I usually make a double batch as it freezes quite nicely. It's a great make-ahead dish. Here at Annabelle's we usually serve it on Sunday mornings."
Ann Mealey – Annabelle's B&B

Blend all above ingredients together. Cover and let sit in the refrigerator for at least 4 hours. Cook in a non-stick 8-inch skillet sprayed with cooking spray. Put a scant 1/3 cup of batter in skillet and rotate pan to spread batter evenly. Lightly brown on both sides. Put layers of waxed paper between cooked crepes if you want to fill later or freeze them. Makes 12 crepes.

Filling
1 (8 oz.) pkg. cream cheese, softened
1 c. ricotta cheese
2 T. powdered sugar
1 1/2 t. vanilla, orange or almond extract
1 1/2 t. orange rind

Combine all of the above ingredients and process until smooth. Place 1 heaping tablespoon of filling in the center of each crepe. Fold to make a square package. They can be frozen at this point. If frozen, it is best to thaw in refrigerator or on counter before cooking. Cook in buttered skillet until browned. Serve immediately with Sauce.

Sauce
3 T. sugar
2 t. cornstarch
1/8 t. cinnamon
1 T. lemon juice
3/4 c. orange juice
1/4 c. creme de cassis (black currant liqueur), optional
1 c. blueberries

Whisk together all of the above ingredients except creme de cassis and blueberries. Cook until thick. Fold in liqueur and berries.

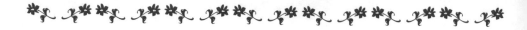

The Tudor Rose

The Tudor Rose is named for the Tudor monarch King Henry VIII. The House of Tudor ruled England from the late 15th century through the 16th century. During the War of the Roses, Henry, who was of the House of Lancaster, defeated the York monarch, Richard III, and was crowned with his fallen crown. Henry married Elizabeth, heir of the House of York, and combined the red rose of Lancaster with the white rose of York to create the Tudor Rose.

INNKEEPERS:	*Jon & Terre' Terrell*
ADDRESS:	*6720 Paradise Road; PO Box 89*
	Salida, CO 81201
TELEPHONE:	*(719) 539-2002; (800) 379-0889*
ROOMS:	*4 Rooms; 2 Suites; Private & shared baths*
OPEN:	*Year-round*
CHILDREN:	*6 years and older welcome*
ANIMALS:	*Welcome; Fenced outdoor accommodations;*
	Overnight stabling
SMOKING:	*No smoking in house or barn*

Seasoned Egg
and Potato Crepes
with Béarnaise Sauce

<u>Crepes</u>
1 c. sifted all-purpose flour
1 1/2 c. milk
2 eggs
1 T. salad oil
1/4 t. salt

In bowl, combine all ingredients. Beat until smooth. Lightly grease and heat a 6-inch skillet or crepe pan. Remove from heat; spoon in about 2 tablespoons of batter. Spread batter evenly. Return to heat; brown on one side for one minute then turn over and cook other side until lightly browned. Grease pan lightly for each crepe. Makes about 12 crepes.

Shortcut: These crepes can be frozen for later use. In the B&B, I like to take a few short cuts when I can to save time. I usually make my crepes the day before and layer parchment paper or waxed paper between the cooled crepes, wrap in plastic and refrigerate. I heat them in the microwave until slightly warm and then fill.

<u>Filling</u>
8 eggs
1/4 c. milk
1/2 t. parsley flakes
1/8 t. Mrs. Dash garlic and herb seasoning
Salt and pepper, to taste
1 1/2 -2 c. diced cooked potatoes

Beat all ingredients together, <u>except</u> potatoes, with a wire whisk until well blended. Add potatoes. Cook in skillet over medium heat until desired doneness. Spoon mixture onto crepes and fold sides of crepes to make a roll. Place seam side down. Makes 4 servings of 2 crepes each.

CONTINUED ON NEXT PAGE....

Béarnaise Sauce
2 shallots, very finely chopped
1 t. tarragon
2 T. wine vinegar
1 t. chopped parsley
3 egg yolks
3/4 lb. unsalted butter, clarified
Salt and freshly ground pepper, to taste

Place shallots, tarragon, vinegar and parsley in stainless steel bowl. Place bowl on stove top over low heat. Cook until vinegar evaporates. Remove from heat and let cool. Add egg yolks and mix well with whisk. Place bowl over saucepan containing hot water. Add clarified butter, drop by drop, mixing constantly with whisk. When sauce begins to thicken, continue to add butter but in a thin stream. Mix constantly with whisk. Season sauce well and serve.

Shortcut: To save time, a package of Knorr's Béarnaise Sauce works just as well. This also can be made the day before and refrigerated. If it is too thick the next day, you can add a little bit of water to thin as you warm it.

Presentation
For this dish I use an orange slice which is then cut with a cookie cutter to remove the rind. On top of that I place a fanned 1/2 strawberry both of which are set on the rim of the dish. Sprinkle parsley flakes all over the plate before putting on the fruit and crepes. Top with Béarnaise sauce spooned over the crepes and all over the plate for decor. Serve with Cherry Filled Crepes on the side. Enjoy!!

Cherry Filled Crepes
4 crepes
1 can Cherry Pie Filling

Warm cherry pie filling in microwave. Warm crepes in microwave. Spoon cherries into center of crepes; fold sides of crepes over top. Spoon extra cherry pie filling on top of crepes allowing it to drizzle onto plate. Serves 4.

FRENCH TOAST
&
GRANOLA

Fireside Inn

An American Youth Hostel during the summer, the Fireside Inn is a converted 1880's Victorian home in Breckenridge's historic Victorian district. Accommodations for this unique bed and breakfast include a suite, rooms with private bathrooms and dorm facilities with shared bathrooms.

A sign in the breakfast room says, "Life is too short not to live in Colorado."

INNKEEPERS:	*Mike & Mary Keeling*
ADDRESS:	*114 North French Street; PO Box 2252*
	Breckenridge, CO 80424
TELEPHONE:	*(970) 453-6456*
	url http://www.colo.com/
	summit/Fireside-Inn
	email: fireside@brecknet.com
ROOMS:	*3 Rooms; 1 Suite; All with private baths*
	5 Dorm rooms; Shared baths
OPEN:	*Year-round*
CHILDREN:	*Children under 12 are free in private rooms*
ANIMALS:	*Prohibited*
SMOKING:	*Prohibited*

Sourdough Cinnamon French Toast

3 eggs
1/8 t. nutmeg
1 t. cinnamon
4 T. milk
Dash of sugar
6 slices sourdough French bread
Maple Syrup (recipe below)

Beat together eggs, nutmeg, cinnamon, milk and sugar. Dip sourdough bread in mixture and cook on a hot, greased griddle or skillet. Serve with Fireside Inn Maple Syrup. Serves 2-3.

<u>Fireside Inn Maple Syrup</u>
2 1/2 c. water
1 lb. light brown sugar
1 1/4 c. white sugar
1 T. maple extract
Dash of vanilla

Mix all ingredients in a saucepan. Bring to a boil, stirring occasionally. Simmer for 30 minutes. Cool. Store leftover syrup in refrigerator. Makes 1 quart.

The House on Ouray

The House on Ouray Bed and Breakfast is a 1905 restored Victorian with three bedrooms – all named after women who made a difference in the history of Colorado. (Molly Brown, Doctor Susan Anderson and Chipeta, wife of Ute Chief Ouray.)

Located in Grand Junction at the junction of the Colorado and Gunnison rivers on the Western Slope of the Rocky Mountains, the city's elevation is 4,586 feet. Originally part of the Ute Indian lands, this area was opened to white settlers in 1880.

INNKEEPERS:	*Arlene & Marlene Johnsen*
ADDRESS:	*760 Ouray Avenue*
	Grand Junction, CO 81501
TELEPHONE:	*(970) 245-8452*
ROOMS:	*3 Rooms; All with private baths*
OPEN:	*Year-round except for December 24, 25 and*
	Thanksgiving Day
CHILDREN:	*Young adults 14 and over are welcome*
ANIMALS:	*Prohibited; Resident dog*
SMOKING:	*Prohibited*

Peaches and Cream French Toast

3 eggs
1 c. light cream or whipping cream
2 T. peach preserves
1/2 t. nutmeg
6 slices French or Italian bread (either in one piece or cut diagonally)
3 T. butter
3 c. fresh, peeled and sliced peaches (use frozen peaches in winter)
Powdered sugar

Combine eggs, cream, peach preserves and nutmeg. Beat until smooth. Dip bread slices in the egg mixture and arrange slices in a single layer in a baking pan. Pour any remaining egg mixture over the bread. Turn the slices to coat evenly. Cover and refrigerate overnight. To cook, melt the butter in a skillet or griddle. Sauté the bread slices until golden brown, about 5 minutes on each side. Top with peaches and sprinkle with powdered sugar.

The Manor

Often referred to as "The Gem of the Rockies," Ouray is a friendly and inviting community. Rich in mining history, the town is a designated *National Historic District.* Many of the Victorian homes and buildings have been faithfully restored to their turn-of-the-century elegance, including The Manor Bed and Breakfast.

Bird watchers are fortunate to see a wide and colorful variety of birds and hummers visiting the garden feeders.

INNKEEPERS:	*Joel & Diane Kramer*
ADDRESS:	*317 Second Street; PO Box 745*
	Ouray, CO 81427
TELEPHONE:	*(970) 325-4574*
ROOMS:	*7 Rooms; All with private baths*
OPEN:	*Year-round*
CHILDREN:	*No small children*
ANIMALS:	*Prohibited*
SMOKING:	*Prohibited*

Upside-Down Apple French Toast

Prepare the night before or at least 3 hours in advance.

1/2 c. (1 stick) butter
1 1/4 c. packed brown sugar
1 T. water
3 Granny Smith apples
Cinnamon, to taste
1/2 c. raisins, optional
1 loaf French bread, sliced 1 1/2-inches thick
1 1/2 c. milk
6 eggs
1 t. vanilla
Nutmeg, to taste
Creme Topping (recipe below)
Sliced almonds, for garnish

Combine butter, brown sugar and water in a saucepan. Heat on medium until bubbling, stirring frequently. Place in a 9x13-inch pan and allow to cool for 20-30 minutes. Peel, core and slice the apples. Place the slices in rows, close together (overlapping), on top of the sauce in pan. Sprinkle with cinnamon and raisins. Place the slices of bread on top of the apples. Mix together the milk, eggs and vanilla. Pour over bread. Sprinkle with a little nutmeg. Cover and refrigerate. Bake at 350° F. for approximately 60 minutes, or until golden brown and crispy on top. Serve upside-down. Spoon the sauce in the pan over the French toast. Serve with Creme Topping and garnish with almonds. Serves 6.

Creme Topping
1/2 c. whipping cream
1/2 c. sour cream
1/4 c. sugar
1/2 t. almond extract

Whip on high until thickened. Place 2 tablespoons of topping on top of French toast.

Ouray 1898 House

In 1896, the discovery of high-grade gold ore by Thomas Walsh prompted the establishment of the Camp Bird Mine south of Ouray. The total value of ores mined exceeded 27 million by 1916. Guests can delight in this bygone era while staying in The Ouray 1898 Bed and Breakfast that was built during this marvelous age.

Guests enjoy the spectacular view of the phenomenal San Juan Mountains from the deck of the inn.

INNKEEPERS:	*Kathy & Lee Bates*
ADDRESS:	*PO Box 641*
	Ouray, CO 81427-0461
TELEPHONE:	*(970) 325-4871; (970) 325-4317*
ROOMS:	*3 Rooms; All with private baths*
OPEN:	*Year-round*
CHILDREN:	*Welcome*
ANIMALS:	*Prohibited*
SMOKING:	*Prohibited*

Ouray Gourmet
Breakfast Bread

6 beaten eggs
1 quart half and half
1/2 c. sugar
1/2 c. Southern Comfort (optional)
1/2 t. cinnamon
1/2 t. nutmeg
1 loaf French bread, cut into 1-inch slices (about 12 slices)

Mix together all ingredients except bread. Dip bread slices into the mixture and put in a 9x13-inch pan (probably will need two pans). Pour remaining mixture over the bread and refrigerate overnight. Before baking the next morning, transfer the slices of bread (letting extra liquid drip off) to a greased insulated cookie sheet, allowing about 1/2 inch between slices. Turn the slices over as you put them on the cookie sheet. Discard any remaining liquid. Bake at 350° F. for approximately 45 minutes, or until puffy and golden brown. Serve with fruit or syrup. Makes 6 servings (2 pieces each).

Posada de Sol y Sombra

Bed and Breakfast

The Posada de Sol y Sombra (Inn of Sun and Shadow) is sequestered behind a white picket fence on a quiet street in the southern Colorado town of LaVeta. This 1890's brick farmhouse is situated at the base of Cuchara Valley between the Sangre de Cristo mountain range and the lofty, skyscraping twin Spanish Peaks.

This area is a haven for artists, photographers, hikers, mountain bikers, fisherman, golfers and history buffs.

INNKEEPERS:	*Betty & Carroll Elwell*
ADDRESS:	*PO Box 522*
	LaVeta, CO 81055
TELEPHONE:	*(719) 742-3159*
ROOMS:	*2 Rooms; Shared bath*
OPEN:	*Year-round*
CHILDREN:	*Welcome*
ANIMALS:	*Please call*
SMOKING:	*Prohibited*

French Toast Sandwiches

8 slices of a dense bread (white, oatmeal raisin, whole wheat)
3 eggs
1/2 c. buttermilk
1/4 t. salt
2 c. cornflakes
4 T. (1/2 stick) butter

Make 4 sandwiches using one of the fillings below. Mix together the eggs, buttermilk and salt in a shallow pan in which you can dip the sandwiches. Crumble the cornflakes slightly and spread them on waxed paper. (We Michiganders might feel compelled to use only Kellogg's or Post Toasties.) Dip (don't soak) both sides of each sandwich in the egg mixture. Then press each side into the cornflakes to coat the bread well. Melt butter on a griddle or skillet on medium heat. Sauté sandwiches until golden brown on each side, turning once. Serve with warm maple syrup and fresh fruit.

Sandwich Filling #1
4 oz. cream cheese, softened
1/4 c. ricotta
Preserves or marmalade

"These sandwiches may be made ahead and frozen. Taken out of the freezer the night before, breakfast is a snap the next morning."
Betty Elwell – Posada de Sol y Sombra

Beat together the 2 cheeses. Divide among 4 slices of bread, spreading to the edges. Dot each cheese topped slice with preserves or marmalade. Top with another slice of bread. May be frozen at this point.

Sandwich Filling #2
4 oz. cream cheese, softened
1/4 c. smooth peanut butter
1 banana, sliced (tossed with 1 T. lemon juice, if desired)

Mix together the cream cheese and peanut butter. Spread on 4 slices of bread. Top with banana slices. Top with another slice of bread. (If to be frozen, leave banana off until time to sauté.)

Shenandoah Inn

The Shenandoah Inn Bed and Breakfast is a recently restored home on two private riverfront acres on the Gold Medal trout waters of the Frying Pan River. Located in Basalt, it offers year-round access to the best of the Colorado outdoors that includes skiing, fishing, biking, white water rafting, golf, tennis and more.

Owner Terri Ziets is a fiber artist. Her work covers the walls of the inn, as well as on the down comforters on the beds.

INNKEEPERS:	*Bob & Terri Ziets*
ADDRESS:	*0600 Frying Pan Road; PO Box 578*
	Basalt, CO 81621
TELEPHONE:	*(970) 927-4991*
ROOMS:	*2 Rooms; 1 Suite; 1 Cabin that sleeps six*
OPEN:	*Year-round*
CHILDREN:	*Well-behaved children over 12 are welcome*
ANIMALS:	*Prohibited*
SMOKING:	*Prohibited*

Orange Crumb
French Toast

2 eggs
1/4 t. salt
2/3 c. fresh orange juice
2 T. Grand Marnier (optional)
3/4 c. corn flake crumbs
3 t. grated orange rind (reserve 1 t. for garnish)
8 (3/4-inch) slices day-old French bread
3 T. sweet butter
Orange Syrup (recipe below)

Combine eggs, salt, orange juice and Grand Marnier with a whisk. Combine cereal crumbs with 2 teaspoons grated orange rind. Dip bread into egg mixture, then dip into cereal crumbs. Coat evenly on all sides. Melt butter in skillet. Brown both sides of bread in butter. Drain on paper towels. Arrange French toast on warm plates, and lightly dust with remaining grated orange rind. Serve with warm Orange Syrup.

<u>Orange Syrup</u>
1 c. Vermont maple syrup
1/4 c. fresh orange juice
1 t. grated orange rind
4 T. sweet butter

Combine syrup ingredients in saucepan. Simmer 5 minutes.

Carol's Corner
The syrup can be made ahead and refrigerated. It can even be frozen. Warm in microwave before serving. Delicious!

St. Mary's Glacier

F rom the deck of this hand-hewn log mountain retreat, guests enjoy majestic views of the Continental Divide, a cascading waterfall and crystalline high mountain lakes. Hiking and cross-country skiing are just outside the front door. In the evening, guests enjoy a romantic suite or roaring fire in the parlor.

Each suite is decorated in comfortable country charm with homemade quilts and exquisite paintings by Colorado artist, Pierre DeBernay.

INNKEEPERS:	*Jackie & Steve Jacquin*
ADDRESS:	*336 Crest Drive*
	Idaho Springs, CO 80452
TELEPHONE:	*(303) 567-4084*
ROOMS:	*5 Suites; All with private baths*
OPEN:	*Year-round*
CHILDREN:	*Not recommended*
ANIMALS:	*Prohibited*
SMOKING:	*Restricted to outdoor areas*

Creme Caramel
French Toast

2 T. corn syrup
1 c. brown sugar
1/2 c. butter
1 1/2 lbs. cinnamon raisin bread
6 eggs
2 c. milk
2 c. light cream
1/3 c. sugar
1 T. vanilla extract
1/2 t. salt
Sour cream

In a saucepan, combine the corn syrup, brown sugar and butter. Melt until smooth and bubbly. Spread in the bottom of a 9x13-inch glass baking dish. Overlap the bread like dominoes on the syrup. In a large bowl, combine the eggs, milk, light cream, sugar, vanilla and salt. Pour the mixture over the bread. Refrigerate the mixture overnight. (Don't be concerned about the extra liquid in the dish; it bakes up like a custard.) Bake <u>covered</u> in a 350° F. oven for 45 minutes, then bake <u>uncovered</u> for 15 minutes more. The toast should be puffed and golden. Cut into 8 pieces and invert to serve. Top each piece with 2 tablespoons (or less) of sour cream, and accompany with fresh berries or a raspberry or cranberry sauce.

Carol's Corner
Creme Caramel French Toast is very moist – something like a bread pudding. This is St. Mary's Glacier B&B's most asked for recipe. Jackie says she oftens prepares it in the morning right before baking and gets the same delicious results.

Sterling House

To enter the front door of Sterling House Bed and Breakfast Inn is to take a step back in time to the ambiance of a bygone era. Guests experience the charm and character of this 1886 home by savoring the warmth and comfort of old wood, deep upholstery and leaded glass.

Sterling House is within walking distance of the University of Northern Colorado, 55 miles north of Denver and one hour's drive to Rocky Mountain National Park.

INNKEEPERS:	*Lillian Peeples*
ADDRESS:	*818 12th Street*
	Greeley, CO 80631
TELEPHONE:	*(970) 351-8805*
ROOMS:	*2 Rooms; Both with private baths*
OPEN:	*Year-round*
CHILDREN:	*Children 10 and older welcome*
ANIMALS:	*Prohibited*
SMOKING:	*Permitted on enclosed porch*

French Toast New Orleans

2 eggs
1/2 c. milk
4 pieces French bread
Oil
Praline Mixture (recipe below)

Combine eggs and milk. Soak the bread in the mixture. Fry the bread in small amount of oil. When cooked on both sides, spread on praline mixture and place frying pan with French toast under the broiler until mixture is bubbling. If your pan is not ovenproof, transfer the toast to a cookie sheet and place under the broiler. May be served with syrup, but not necessary. Serves 2.

Praline Mixture
1/4 c. brown sugar
1/8 c. chopped pecans
1 T. butter
1 t. vanilla

Combine all ingredients in a non-metal bowl and warm in microwave or heat on stove. Stir until ingredients are mixed and smooth.

Sunflower

L ocated at the base of the LaPlata Mountains in Southwest Colorado, the Sunflower Bed and Breakfast is country living at its finest. This large country inn, nestled in a wildflower garden, affords panoramic views of ancient mountains and mesas.

Local attractions include the historic Durango and the Narrow Gauge Railroad, Mesa Verde National Park and the Anasazi ruins. Sports enthusiasts enjoy rafting, skiing and biking.

INNKEEPERS:	*Chris Isgar & Jackson Seay*
ADDRESS:	*10829 C.R. 141*
	Hesperus, CO 81326
TELEPHONE:	*(970) 385-4534*
ROOMS:	*2 Rooms; 1 Suite; 1 separate Southwestern house with private gardens*
OPEN:	*Year-round*
CHILDREN:	*Welcome*
ANIMALS:	*Prohibited*
SMOKING:	*Prohibited*

Sunflower's Baked French Toast

1 loaf French bread, unsliced
8 oz. cream cheese, softened
1 c. powdered sugar
10 eggs
3/4 c. table cream or milk
1 t. vanilla extract
Cinnamon-sugar mixture, optional

"Buffet breakfast at the Sunflower is served with views of the Sleeping Ute, La Plata Mountains, and don't be surprised if the deer or elk beg for a bite, too."
Chris Isgar – Sunflower B&B

Remove the outer crust of French bread with a sharp serrated knife – this will enable the egg mixture to soak into the bread better. Cut bread lengthwise (like a sandwich). In a small bowl, mix softened cream cheese with the powdered sugar. Spread this mixture on the bottom piece of bread and then place the other piece of bread on top. In a large bowl, mix eggs, cream or milk and vanilla. Pour the mixture into a 9x13-inch baking dish. Add French bread, turning several times in egg mixture. Sprinkle cinnamon-sugar on top, if desired. Cover with plastic wrap and place in refrigerator overnight. When ready to bake, place soaked bread on a buttered cookie sheet. Bake at 375° F. for 25 minutes, or until golden brown. Serve with syrup of your choice or Strawberry Sauce. Makes 8 servings.

<u>Strawberry Sauce</u>
1 quart hulled strawberries (or berries of your choice)
1/3 c. sugar
2 T. water
2 T. orange flavored liqueur (optional)

Cook all ingredients in a pan over medium heat for 5 minutes. Remove sauce from heat and pour over French toast.

Crystal Inn

The Crystal Inn Bed and Breakfast, located in historic Crested Butte, is filled with American antiques, including a working, antique telephone. Each guest room in this quiet, but inviting inn is tastefully decorated with quilts, comforters, coordinated linens and window treatments.

"No one goes away hungry," says Charlene, who opened the inn with her husband, Dennis after she retired as a nurse in Houston. Dennis, a retiree from Southwestern Bell in Houston, built the Crystal Inn.

INNKEEPERS:	*Dennis & Charlene Goree*
ADDRESS:	*624 Gothic Avenue; PO Box 125*
	Crested Butte, CO 81224
TELEPHONE:	*(970) 349-1338; (800) 390-1338*
ROOMS:	*5 Rooms; All with private baths*
OPEN:	*Year-round*
CHILDREN:	*Childen 12 and older are welcome*
ANIMALS:	*Prohibited*
SMOKING:	*Prohibited*

Crystal Inn French Toast

5 eggs, beaten
1 (12 oz.) can evaporated milk
1 c. sugar
1 t. cinnamon
1 1/2 T. vanilla extract (not imitation)
1/4 c. margarine, melted
1 large loaf French bread

Mix eggs with milk. Add sugar, cinnamon and vanilla. Mix in melted margarine. Cut bread into 3/4-inch pieces. Dip bread in egg mixture and place on 350° F. griddle or on medium high skillet. Grill until brown on both sides. Place on serving platter and dust with powdered sugar. Serves 8-10.

"This is our most requested item for breakfast. We might serve this with bacon, fresh fruit and Devonshire cream."
Charlene Goree – Crystal Inn B&B

St. Elmo Hotel

G uests step back in time and relive the glory days of Colorado's colorful past at the St. Elmo Hotel in Ouray, Colorado. Once bustling with gold and silver seekers, Ouray today is a picturesque hamlet, nestled in the majestic San Juan mountains of southwestern Colorado.

Furnished with antiques, stained glass, polished wood and brass trim throughout, the St. Elmo Hotel offers a charming lobby, cozy parlor and sunny breakfast room.

INNKEEPERS:	*Dan & Sandy Lingenfelter*
ADDRESS:	*426 Main Street; PO Box 667*
	Ouray, CO 81427
TELEPHONE:	*(970) 325-4951*
ROOMS:	*9 Rooms; All with private baths*
OPEN:	*Year-round*
CHILDREN:	*Welcome*
ANIMALS:	*Prohibited*
SMOKING:	*Restricted to outdoors*

Orange French Toast

6 eggs
1 c. orange juice
1/3 c. milk
1/4 t. vanilla extract
1/4 t. salt
Peel of 1 orange, finely grated
12 slices French bread, 3/4-inch thick

Beat eggs in a large bowl. Add orange juice, milk, vanilla, salt and orange peel. Mix well. Dip bread in egg mixture, turning to coat all sides. Place on a baking sheet in a single layer. Pour any remaining egg mixture over the top – turn pieces over a couple of times. Cover with plastic wrap and put in refrigerator overnight. Fry pieces on oiled griddle or skillet until golden brown. Serve with maple syrup. Makes 6 servings.

Gunbarrel Guest House

The Gunbarrel Guest House boasts tastefully decorated suites with fireplaces, kitchenettes and private baths. Some suites include a separate sitting room with private whirlpool bath. Complimentary beverages are provided daily.

The Guest House is near Boulder County's industrial and residential areas and major highways. The full-service conference and meeting rooms are ideal for weekend retreats, seminars and all types of meetings.

INNKEEPERS:	*Carolann Evans*
ADDRESS:	*6901 Lookout Road*
	Boulder, CO 80301
TELEPHONE:	*(303) 530-1513*
ROOMS:	*13 Rooms; All with private baths*
OPEN:	*Year-round*
CHILDREN:	*Welcome*
ANIMALS:	*Please call before bringing animals*
SMOKING:	*Prohibited*

Guest House Granola

5 c. rolled oats
1 1/2 c. shelled sunflower seeds
1 1/2 c. wheat germ
1 1/2 c. shredded coconut
1 1/2 c. flaked bran (or All Bran)
1 1/2 c. chopped pecans
1 1/2 c. chopped walnuts
1 1/2 c. slivered almonds
3/4 c. sesame seeds

Mix all of the above ingredients in a very large bowl and set aside.

3/4 c. vegetable or canola oil
3/4 c. honey
3/4 c. molasses
1 1/2 t. almond flavoring
1 1/2 t. vanilla flavoring

In a saucepan, bring the above 5 ingredients to a boil and cook for 4 minutes (or until thoroughly blended). Pour slowly over the dry ingredients in the bowl. Place all ingredients evenly on two sheet pans and put in 350° F. oven. Let toast for 5-8 minutes. Take out of oven and stir all ingredients. Place back in oven for 4 minutes; bring out and stir. Repeat 3 or 4 more times. Watch carefully, so it doesn't get too brown. Cool thoroughly and sprinkle with raisins. Note: If granola clumps, try placing it back in the oven and toast a bit more.

"The above recipe was brought to the Guest House by the very first innkeeper here in 1986. It is so popular and the requests for the recipe were so numerous, we finally had it printed. We also have several local businessmen that buy it regularly to have at home."
Carolann Evans – Gunbarrel Guest House

Thompson House Inn

T he Quilting Bee room at the Thompson House Inn reminds guests of Grandmother's house. "Granny's" attic room is decorated with a double white iron bed with patchwork quilts, a Victorian rocking chair and nostalgic photographs.

The Victorian Rose room was inspired by the grace of the Victorian era. This elegant room showcases a large antique queen-size bed, Duncan Phyfe love seat and marble fireplace with an exquisite antique mantle.

INNKEEPERS:	*Sheila Merrill & Marvin Bonta*
ADDRESS:	*537 Terry Street*
	Longmont, CO 80501
TELEPHONE:	*(303) 651-6675*
ROOMS:	*7 Rooms; All with private baths*
OPEN:	*Year-round*
CHILDREN:	*Children over the age of 10 are welcome*
ANIMALS:	*Prohibited*
SMOKING:	*Smoking in outdoor areas only*

Deborah's Granola

1 c. brown sugar
1/3 c. vegetable oil
1/4 c. molasses
1/2 c. honey
2 1/2 T. cinnamon
1 c. water

In a medium saucepan, whisk together all of the above ingredients and heat to a simmer. Set aside to cool.

8 c. oatmeal
2 T. sesame seeds
1/4 c. wheat germ
1 c. walnut pieces
1 c. pecan pieces
1 c. almonds, sliced
1 c. coconut
1 c. shelled sunflower seeds, raw
2 1/2 c. raisins

In a very large bowl, mix all of the above ingredients <u>except</u> raisins. Add wet ingredients to the dry ingredients and mix thoroughly. Split mixture onto 2 sheet pans and place in 250° F. oven. Stir every 20 minutes for about 2 1/2 hours, or until toasted and dry. Allow to cool and add 1 1/4 cup raisins per sheet pan. Mix and store in jars.

"The granola is not only a favorite to eat, but the aroma in the Inn while we're cooking is wonderful!"
Marvin Bonta – The Thompson House Inn

EGG
ENTRÉES

Alpen Rose

The superb views of James and Perry Peaks from the large southern deck of the Alpen Rose Bed and Breakfast Inn are often embraced by spectacular sunrises and evening alpen glows. The breathtaking view is enhanced by lofty pines, wildflowers and quaking aspens.

Robin Sommerauer, the host, is a licensed mountain climber who was a member of an expedition of women that made an assault on the Himalayan peak of Dhaulagiri.

INNKEEPERS:	*Robin & Rupert Sommerauer*
ADDRESS:	*244 Forest Trail; PO Box 769*
	Winter Park, CO 80482
TELEPHONE:	*(970) 726-5039; (800) 531-1373*
ROOMS:	*4 Rooms; 1 Suite; All with private baths*
OPEN:	*Mid-November through Mid-September*
CHILDREN:	*Welcome*
ANIMALS:	*Prohibited*
SMOKING:	*Prohibited*

Crustless Quiche

1/2 c. butter (1 stick)
1/2 c. all-purpose flour
6 large eggs, beaten
1 c. milk
16 oz. Monterey Jack cheese, shredded
1 (3 oz.) pkg. cream cheese, softened
2 c. cottage cheese
1 t. baking powder
1 t. salt
1 t. sugar

Preheat oven to 350° F. Melt butter in a saucepan. Add flour and cook until smooth. In a large bowl, beat eggs. Add cooked mixture and remaining ingredients. Stir until well blended. Pour into a well greased 9x13-inch pan. Bake uncovered for 45 minutes.

Carol's Corner

This is divine! A light, delicate flavor...practically melts in your mouth!

The Gothic Inn

The Gothic Inn Bed and Breakfast is nestled among the tall mountains and gentle valleys in Colorado's intimate, friendly town of Crested Butte. Surrounded by unspoiled, accessible beauty, the inn is ideally placed as home base for many forms of outdoor and social recreation.

This large, modern-equipped oak house offers European hospitality. Each room is furnished in antique-style, hand-painted furniture.

INNKEEPERS:	*Sonja Ruta*
ADDRESS:	*PO Box 1488*
	Crested Butte, CO 81224
TELEPHONE:	*(970) 349-7215*
ROOMS:	*5 Rooms; Private and shared baths*
OPEN:	*Year-round*
CHILDREN:	*Welcome*
ANIMALS:	*Prohibited*
SMOKING:	*Prohibited*

Vegetable Burrito

3 green onions, sliced
1 strip bacon, cut in pieces (optional)
4 small zucchini, grated (use largest holes on grater)
Provincial Spice
Salt
3 eggs
4 flour tortillas
Cheddar cheese, shredded
Swiss cheese, shredded
Salsa
Sour cream
Red pepper, chopped, for garnish
Parsley, chopped, for garnish

Sauté onion and bacon for several minutes. Add grated zucchini and continue to <u>lightly</u> sauté; zucchini should stay crisp-tender. Season with Provincial Spice and salt, to taste. Meanwhile, scramble the eggs. Moisten the tortillas slightly and heat in microwave a few seconds so they become soft and rollable. Fill the tortillas with the zucchini mixture and eggs and sprinkle with both kinds of cheese. Roll up. Put some salsa and more of both cheeses on top of the rolled up tortillas. Bake in oven at 350° F. until the cheese melts. Serve hot, topped with a little sour cream and garnished with chopped red pepper and parsley.

Carol's Corner
Sonja Ruta at the Gothic Inn says that Provincial Spice is a European blend. If you are unable to locate it in your grocery store, try any herb seasoning mixture that contains several of the following spices found in Provincial Spice – sage, thyme, marjoram, savory, rosemary, tarragon, and basil.

The Hardy House

Built in the late 1800's, The Hardy House is located in the heart of the Historic District in Georgetown. The Romance Package welcomes guests with flowers, chocolates and chilled spirits. A carriage ride delivers them to a restaurant in Georgetown for dinner. Welcoming morning treats include Eggs Benedict, Crab Puffs or Belgian Waffles.

The Skiers Package includes one to three days at the Hardy House, daily lift tickets for two at Loveland and a delicious breakfast in the room.

INNKEEPERS:	*Carla & Mike Wagner*
ADDRESS:	*605 Brownell Street; PO Box 156*
	Georgetown, CO 80444
TELEPHONE:	*(303) 569-3388; (800) 490-4802*
ROOMS:	*2 Rooms; 2 Suites; All with private baths*
OPEN:	*Year-round*
CHILDREN:	*Children over 12 are welcome*
ANIMALS:	*Prohibited; Resident bird*
SMOKING:	*Prohibited*

Smoked Turkey Puffs

1 lb. smoked turkey, chopped
1 1/2 c. Cheddar cheese, finely shredded
12 eggs
2 c. milk
Dash garlic salt
Dash Worcestershire sauce
Sour cream
Fresh ground pepper

Spray 6 individual bowls or egg cups, 4-inches in diameter, with cooking spray. Divide the turkey equally in each bowl and then add 1/4 cup cheese to each. Place the eggs, milk, garlic salt and Worcestershire sauce in a blender. Blend until frothy. Pour egg mixture (about 1 cupful per bowl) over cheese. Bowls will be quite full. Drop 1 tablespoon sour cream on top. Add some fresh ground pepper. Bake at 350° F. approximately 30-45 minutes or until browned and puffed. Makes 6 servings.

Carol's Corner

If you do not already have a pepper mill or grinder, look for the new Spice Islands black pepper grinder in the spice aisle of your grocery store. It's just the perfect size to keep by the stove, and you'll always have freshly ground pepper at your fingertips.

Holden House - 1902

T his storybook, Colonial Revival Victorian home and carriage house
was built in 1902 by Mrs. Isabel Holden, widow of rancher and
businessman Daniel M. Holden. The Holdens owned mining interests in
Aspen, Cripple Creek, Leadville, Silverton, Goldfield and Independence.

The Holden House - 1902 Bed and Breakfast Inn was restored in the mid-
1980's and has been filled with the Clarks' antiques and family
heirlooms.

INNKEEPERS: *Sallie & Welling Clark*
ADDRESS: *1102 W. Pikes Peak Avenue*
Colorado Springs, CO 80904
TELEPHONE: *(719) 471-3980*
ROOMS: *2 Rooms; 4 Suites; All with private baths*
OPEN: *Year-round*
CHILDREN: *Prohibited*
ANIMALS: *Prohibited; 2 Resident cats*
SMOKING: *Prohibited*

Southwestern Eggs Fiesta

24 eggs (2 eggs per person)
12 oz. cheddar cheese (1 oz. per person)
Bacon bits or crumbled cooked turkey bacon
Sour cream for topping
Mild picante sauce for topping
6 snack size flour tortillas, cut in half (1/2 tortilla per person)
Parsley, for garnish
Cilantro (fresh, if available)

Thoroughly grease 12 individual soufflé dishes (5-8 oz. size) with non-stick cooking spray. Break 2 eggs into each dish. Place 1/2 tortilla in each dish, flat edge down and outside of eggs to form a U-shape around edge of dish. Top eggs with 1 oz. of cheese and some crumbled bacon or bacon bits. Sprinkle with a dash of cilantro. Bake at 375° F. for 20-30 minutes or until eggs are done, cheese is melted and tortilla is slightly brown. Top with a dab of sour cream and a teaspoon of picante sauce. Sprinkle a dash of cilantro on top and place on a serving plate. Garnish with additional parsley, if desired. Serves 12, but can easily be adapted for more or fewer persons.

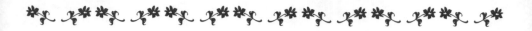

Hughes Hacienda

Hughes Hacienda sits high on a hill at the foot of Blue Mountain outside of Colorado Springs. Guests enjoy magnificent views of the Rocky Mountains, Red Rock Valley and the twinkling of evening lights from Colorado Springs.

Abundant wildlife inhabits the secluded 19 acre compound, including deer, raccoon, fox and birds. Guests can hike the well-maintained trails or simply relax in the portal overlooking the mountains and valley below.

INNKEEPERS: *Wayne & Carol Hughes*
ADDRESS: *12060 Calle Corvo*
Colorado Springs, CO 80926
TELEPHONE: *(719) 576-2060*
ROOMS: *1 Suite; Private bath*
OPEN: *Year-round*
CHILDREN: *Prohibited*
ANIMALS: *Prohibited*
SMOKING: *Prohibited*

Breakfast Rellenos

2 Anaheim chiles (also called New Mexico #6)
1 T. piñon nuts (raw)
1 T. golden raisins
4 T. sour cream
1/2 c. Farmers cheese, grated
2 eggs
4 slices avocado, for garnish

Place chiles on a foil-covered cookie sheet. Place 4-6 inches below the broiler unit. Roast chiles for 6-8 minutes, rotating occasionally, until lightly charred and uniformly blistered. Remove from the broiler and place in a plastic bag and close tightly. Steam for 5 minutes. Remove from bag and wash under cold water to remove the skin. Leave the stems on. Make a slit lengthwise in the chile and remove the seeds. Pat dry with paper towel and place on an oven-proof plate, slit side up. Roast piñon nuts in a small iron skillet over low heat until light brown. Stir often to prevent scorching. Scramble the eggs with piñon nuts and raisins. Spoon egg mixture into the prepared chiles. Spoon sour cream over eggs and sprinkle cheese on top. Place under the broiler until cheese melts. Place on serving dish and garnish with avocado slices. Serve with hashbrown potatoes, a meat and an assortment of fresh fruit.

Carol's Corner
Piñon is Spanish for pine. Pine nuts are also called pignolias. (Pignolias are shelled pine nuts.) The nuts are removed from the insides of pine cones.

The Mary Lawrence Inn

Located in a quiet, residential neighborhood, the Mary Lawrence Inn offers its guests a restful stay, the quiet majesty of the mountains and nature at its best. The inn is perfectly located for a variety of recreational activities including skiing at Crested Butte and Monarch Resort, Gold Medal fishing on the Taylor, East or Gunnison Rivers, mountain biking and hiking.

Gunnison offers a full-service airport. (One of the busiest on the Western Slope.)

INNKEEPERS:	*Pat & Jim Kennedy*
ADDRESS:	*601 North Taylor*
	Gunnison, CO 81230
TELEPHONE:	*(970) 641-3343*
ROOMS:	*4 Rooms; 1 Suite; All with private baths*
OPEN:	*Year-round*
CHILDREN:	*Ages six and older are welcome*
ANIMALS:	*Prohibited; Two resident cats*
SMOKING:	*Prohibited*

Mediterranean Eggs

8 eggs, beaten
8 T. sour cream (low fat works fine)
8 sun-dried tomatoes, reconstituted and chopped
1 ripe tomato, chopped
Basil pesto (purchased)
1/8 c. green onions, sliced
3-4 oz. feta cheese, crumbled
Black olives, sliced
Pine nuts
Basil leaves, for garnish

Cream Sauce
1 T. butter or margarine
2 T. flour
1 c. warm milk
Salt and pepper, to taste

> *Carol's Corner*
> *This is great! The contrast between the red, green, black and white colors makes this a very pretty dish. You can easily decrease or increase the amounts of the ingredients to make the right number of servings for your guests.*

Make cream sauce: Melt butter in small saucepan. Whisk in flour, stirring over low heat until bubbly. Slowly whisk in warm milk and stir over medium heat until thick and bubbling. Add salt and pepper. Set aside.

In skillet, <u>slowly</u> scramble eggs in a small amount of butter (or use cooking spray) until cooked but moist. Mix in cream sauce. Divide mixture among 4 ramekins or small au gratin dishes coated with cooking spray. Dot with sour cream. Sprinkle with both kinds of tomatoes, pesto to taste, green onions and feta cheese. Top with black olives and pine nuts. Bake at 350° F. for 10-15 minutes. Remove from oven and garnish with fresh basil leaves. Serve piping hot. Serves 4.

"While you would never be served this dish anywhere in the Mediterranean, (certainly not for breakfast), we love its sunny flavors that take us back to warm, fragrant places we have visited. One can almost see the coast from our window."
Pat and Jim Kennedy – Mary Lawrence Inn

Meister House

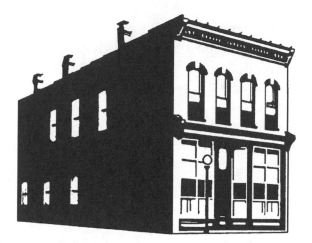

Originally built in the 1890's as a small, first-class hotel for the weary mining, ranching and railroad executives, this revitalized two-story brick structure is located in central Colorado. The Upper Arkansas River Valley and Collegiate Mountain Range are within walking distance.

In the mornings, guests watch the sun rise over Sleeping Indian Mountain from the sun-drenched courtyard before savoring a hearty gourmet breakfast with all the trimmings.

INNKEEPERS:	*Barbara & Frank Hofmeister*
ADDRESS:	*414 East Main Street; PO Box 1133*
	Buena Vista, CO 81211
TELEPHONE:	*(719) 395-9220; (800) 882-1821*
ROOMS:	*7 Rooms; All with private baths*
OPEN:	*Year-round*
CHILDREN:	*Children welcome over the age of 10*
ANIMALS:	*Prohibited*
SMOKING:	*Prohibited*

Crab Scramble

2 T. butter
9 eggs, beaten
1/2 c. milk
2 (3 oz.) pkg. cream cheese, cubed
1 (6 1/2 oz.) can crab meat
1/2 t. salt
1/4 t. pepper
1 T. chopped fresh baby dill (use smaller amount if using dried dill)

In an 8x11.5-inch pan melt the butter. In a large bowl, combine eggs, milk, cream cheese, crab meat, salt and pepper. Pour the mixture over the melted butter and sprinkle with dill. Bake in 350° F. oven for 30 minutes. Serves 6-8.

For a low fat version, substitute a 6 oz. package of imitation crab for real crab, use low fat cream cheese and an egg substitute. Non-stick cooking spray can be used in place of butter.

The Painted Lady

Built in 1894, The Painted Lady Bed and Breakfast Inn was home to William Proctor, the proprietor of the local billiard hall. This three-story, fanciful Victorian (complete with gingerbread trim, coach lights on the wraparound balcony and six colors of paint) makes it a true "Painted Lady."

"Thanks for everything. Your home was one of the great experiences we had in the United States."

~ Guest from Switzerland

INNKEEPERS:	*Valerie & Zan Maslowski*
ADDRESS:	*1318 W. Colorado Avenue*
	Colorado Springs, CO 80904
TELEPHONE:	*(719) 473-3165; (800) 370-3165*
ROOMS:	*2 Rooms; 2 Suites; All with private baths*
OPEN:	*Year-round*
CHILDREN:	*Children over eight-years-old can be accommodated in the suite*
ANIMALS:	*Prohibited; Resident cat*
SMOKING:	*Prohibited*

Crab and Artichoke Egg Puff

5 eggs, beaten
1/4 c. flour
1/2 t. baking powder
8 oz. cottage cheese
2 c. Monterey Jack cheese, grated
4 oz. crab or imitation crab, shredded
6 oz. artichoke hearts, chopped

Combine all ingredients. Spray 4 individual ovenproof bowls (approximately 5" in diameter) with cooking spray. Divide mixture into the bowls. Bake at 350° F. for approximately 30 minutes, or until golden brown. Serve with sliced or cubed baked potatoes topped with sherried cream sauce. Garnish plate with fresh fruit.

Piney Acres Inn

Nestled in the pines of Dillon, Piney Acres Inn offers the beauty, tranquillity and hospitality of a mountain bed and breakfast. Originally built as a log-clad private home, the inn has recently been updated to provide modern amenities while preserving the charm and warmth of a mountain retreat.

After a day of mountain activity or sightseeing, guests can enjoy listening to a pianist who plays the grand piano in the great room.

INNKEEPERS: *Judith McVeigh*
ADDRESS: *864 Anemone Trail; PO Box 4016*
Dillon, CO 80435
TELEPHONE: *(970) 468-6206; (800) 746-3969*
ROOMS: *10 Rooms; All with private baths*
OPEN: *Year-round*
CHILDREN: *Children over the age of 12 are welcome*
ANIMALS: *Prohibited; However, boarding kennels are nearby*
SMOKING: *Prohibited*

Iowa Eggs Benedict

3/4 c. butter (1 1/2 sticks)
3/4 c. all-purpose flour
4 c. milk
2 lb. ham, cubed
1 1/2 c. cheddar cheese, grated
12 eggs, hard-boiled and cubed
1 lb. asparagus, cut into 1-inch pieces, blanched
Spice Islands Beau Monde seasoning, to taste (start with 1/2 t.)
1/2-3/4 c. cooking sherry

> **Carol's Corner**
> *If you do not have Beau Monde seasoning, substitute with a small amount of salt, onion salt, and celery salt.*

Make a white sauce: Melt butter in a large saucepan over moderate heat. Blend in flour. Cook, stirring constantly, until mixture is smooth and bubbly. Gradually add milk. Heat to boiling, stirring constantly. Turn heat to low. Add ham and cheese. Stir until cheese is melted. Add eggs and asparagus. Stir in seasoning and sherry. Stir very gently while heating thoroughly. Serve over Sweet Corn Bread. Serves 6-8.

<u>Sweet Corn Bread</u> (alterations made for high altitude)
2 c. plus 4 T. sifted all-purpose flour
2 c. yellow corn meal
6 t. baking powder
1 t. salt
1/2 c. sugar
4 eggs, slightly beaten
2 c. plus 4 T. milk
6 T. butter or margarine, melted
2 small cans (8 3/4 oz. each) creamed corn

Preheat oven to 425° F. Grease a 9x13-inch glass baking pan. Sift flour, corn meal, baking powder, salt and sugar. Set aside. In a large bowl, combine eggs, milk, butter and corn. Add flour mixture and stir until moistened. Spoon batter into pan. Bake 25-30 minutes, or until cake tester comes out clean and top is golden brown.

Alpen Rose

Hidden away just minutes from downtown Winter Park, the Alpen Rose Bed and Breakfast boasts of "Austrian warmth and hospitality." A large deck off the lodge's common room affords a panoramic view highlighted by the backside of the majestic Front Range.

Each of the four bedrooms is exquisitely decorated with treasures brought from Austria, including traditional featherbeds.

INNKEEPERS:	*Robin & Rupert Sommerauer*
ADDRESS:	*244 Forest Trail; PO Box 769*
	Winter Park, CO 80482
TELEPHONE:	*(970) 726-5039; (800) 531-1373*
ROOMS:	*4 Rooms; 1 Suite; All with private baths*
OPEN:	*Mid-November through Mid-September*
CHILDREN:	*Children are welcome*
ANIMALS:	*Prohibited*
SMOKING:	*Prohibited*

Alpen Rose Baked Eggs

10 oz. pork breakfast sausage
10 eggs, beaten
1/3 c. all-purpose flour
3/4 t. baking powder
16 oz. (4 c.) Monterey Jack cheese, shredded
12 oz. (1 1/2 c.) cottage cheese
3/4 c. fresh mushrooms, sliced or chopped

Preheat oven to 375° F. Cook sausage in a skillet. Drain and crumble. Set aside. Beat eggs, flour and baking powder together. Add sausage, cheeses and mushrooms. Mix well. Pour into a greased 9x13-inch glass baking dish. Bake for 35-40 minutes. Serves 10.

TLC's

According to owner Mary Jo Coulehan, TLC does not stand for "Tender Loving Care". It stands for the initials of her parents, Tom and Lottie Coulehan. Mary Jo lost them both within a short period of time. Since they loved the outdoors, and traveling, Mary Jo thought it appropriate to name her dream after them.

When Mary Jo bought the house, Ayla, a dog, came with the purchase. Due to Ayla's loving nature, one small girl got over her fear of dogs.

INNKEEPERS: *Mary Jo Coulehan*
ADDRESS: *PO Box 3337*
Pagosa Springs, CO 81147
TELEPHONE: *(970) 264-6200; (800) 788-5090*
ROOMS: *2 Rooms; 3 Suites*
OPEN: *Year-round*
CHILDREN: *Welcome*
ANIMALS: *Prohibited; Horseboarding is available with prior notice only*
SMOKING: *Prohibited*

Scrambled Eggs
with Herb Cheese

2 oz. cream cheese
1-2 t. crushed basil
Pinch of thyme
8 eggs
2 T. milk, approximately
1-2 T. butter or margarine
Options: Chopped onions, mushrooms, green chiles, ham

In a small bowl, mix cream cheese, basil and thyme. In a medium bowl, scramble eggs and add milk. In skillet, melt butter. Sauté any of the options listed, depending on your guests' tastes. Add the eggs and cook. When almost fully cooked, add the cream cheese mixture and melt the cheese thoroughly through the eggs. Serve immediately. Serves 4-5.

"The great treat of this recipe is that it is super easy, great for a pop-up breakfast, and most of the items you already have on hand. I get rave reviews on the cream cheese mixture. It's much better than what you can buy in the store and it's so easy to make. In addition, this recipe can be adjusted to fit the number of people that you are serving. Enjoy!"
Mary Jo Coulehan – TLC's: A Bed & Breakfast

The Van Horn House

Located in Roaring Fork Valley, The Van Horn House at Lions Ridge Bed and Breakfast is within minutes of Aspen, Snowmass and Ski Sunlight ski areas. Nearby are the historic towns of Redstone, Marble and Glenwood Springs, home of the world famous hot springs pool.

Each of the four guest rooms has been furnished with antiques, lace curtains, stained glass and just plain charm and coziness!

INNKEEPERS: *John & Susan Laatsch*
ADDRESS: *0318 Lions Ridge Road*
Carbondale, CO 81623
TELEPHONE: *(970) 963-3605*
ROOMS: *4 Rooms; Two with private balconies*
OPEN: *Year-round*
CHILDREN: *Children over 8 are welcome*
ANIMALS: *Prohibited; Resident cat*
SMOKING: *Prohibited*

Susan's Wake-Up Eggs

6 large eggs
1/4 c. minced scallion
1/2 t. salt, or to taste
1/2 t. pepper, or to taste
Dash cayenne pepper, or to taste (optional)
1/4-1/3 c. real mayonnaise (can use low-fat)
4 Australian Toaster Biscuits (preferably corn bread flavor) <u>OR</u>
4 thick English muffins (preferably Wolfram's), cut in half
8 t. unsalted butter (do not use margarine)
8 t. honey
8 slices Canadian bacon or ham, cut 1/4-inch thick
(I often use turkey ham for a lower fat content)
Cheese of your choice, finely grated (I particularly like to use a
seasoned "taco" cheese mix found already grated in the dairy case)

Hard cook the eggs, peel and chop. Add scallions, salt, pepper and cayenne
if being used. Moisten with mayonnaise, using more if the mixture seems
dry. This can be prepared the night before serving and refrigerated. (Actually
better if you do – it lets the flavors blend.) Stir before using. Toast the
biscuits or muffins until medium brown. Watch carefully – do not overtoast.
Spread each half with 1 t. of butter and 1 t. honey. Top with one slice of
ham. Spread egg mixture on top of ham and top generously with cheese.
Heat oven to 350° F. Place biscuit halves on baking sheet and heat for 10 to
12 minutes, or until cheese is melted and egg mixture begins to bubble.
Grilled pineapple slices are a tasty accompaniment to this recipe. Serves 4.

*"This is a wonderful recipe since it can be increased or decreased easily, can be quickly
varied, perhaps with what you have on hand, and can be made at least partially in
advance. There is no reason that you can't use bacon instead of ham, or that you can't
add mushrooms or another vegetable if you wish, or use different cheeses, or leave out
the cayenne and add herbs. It's a fun recipe because it allows you to let your
imagination run!"*
Susan Laatsch – The Van Horn House at Lions Ridge B&B

West Pawnee Ranch

The West Pawnee Ranch Bed and Breakfast is a working ranch located on the peaceful prairie in northeastern Colorado. Guests can participate in ranch routines that include moving cattle, branding or calving. They can also ride along with the owners as they check cattle, fences and water wells.

The ranch is 20 miles from the nearest cafe, so the owners offer additional meals. A Beef Kabob recipe is a favorite and was featured in the July 1995 issue of *Redbook* magazine.

INNKEEPERS: *Paul & Louanne Timm*
ADDRESS: *29451 Weld County Road 130*
    Grover, CO 80729
TELEPHONE: *(970) 895-2482*
ROOMS: *2 Rooms; Both with private baths*
OPEN: *Year-round*
CHILDREN: *Children are always welcome!*
ANIMALS: *Prohibited*
SMOKING: *Prohibited*

WPR Frittata

1 or 2 (7 oz.) cans diced green chiles
6 flour tortillas
4 c. (16 oz.) Monterey Jack cheese
10 large eggs
3/4 c. half and half
1/2 t. ground cumin
1/2 t. onion salt
1/2 t. garlic salt
1/2 t. black pepper
1/2 t. salt

Lightly oil a 9x13-inch casserole dish. Spread one can of green chiles on the bottom of the pan. (Or 1/2 can if using just one can). Top with 3 of the tortillas, tearing or cutting them into 1"x1" pieces. Add 2 cups of the cheese. Repeat layers (chiles, tortillas, cheese). Whisk eggs and half and half together. Add all spices to egg mixture and mix well. Slowly pour egg mixture over entire top layer. Cover with foil and refrigerate overnight. Preheat oven to 350° F. Remove foil from baking dish and bake 45 minutes or until lightly browned and bubbly. Cool slightly and cut into serving pieces. Serve with picante sauce. Serves 8.

Carol's Corner

A delicious and easy way to serve a crowd! For a small gathering, this recipe can easily be cut in half and baked in a 7x11-inch casserole dish for 30-35 minutes. Makes 4 large servings.

Woodland Inn

W oodland Inn Bed and Breakfast is a cozy country inn with fantastic views of Pikes Peak. Peacefully secluded on 12 acres of woodlands, guests enjoy viewing the abundant wildlife. The inn is available for small weddings, receptions and retreats and can accommodate small meetings.

Frank, the owner, is an FAA certified hot air balloon pilot and will take guests for an exciting morning of ballooning.

INNKEEPERS:	*Frank & Nancy O'Neil*
ADDRESS:	*159 Trull Road*
	Woodland Park, CO 80863
TELEPHONE:	*(719) 687-8209; (800) 226-9565*
ROOMS:	*7 Rooms; All with private baths; 1 Room available for disabled persons*
OPEN:	*Year-round*
CHILDREN:	*Children with well-behaved parents are welcome*
ANIMALS:	*Prohibited; Resident dog and cat*
SMOKING:	*Permitted outdoors only*

Frank's Seafood Omelette

2 T. butter or margarine
8 green onions, chopped
2 c. fresh mushrooms, sliced
1 dozen shrimp, medium size, cooked and halved lengthwise
   (set aside 4 halves for garnish)
8 oz. crab meat, cooked or imitation
1/2 c. sour cream
8 eggs (2 per omelette)
1-2 c. grated Swiss cheese
Parsley, for garnish

Melt butter in skillet and sauté onions and mushrooms until soft. Add cooked seafood, setting aside 4 shrimp halves to be used for garnish. Add sour cream. Stir together and warm over very low temperature and set aside. (Do not allow sour cream to boil.) Whip eggs (2 at a time) and pour into a buttered 8-inch omelette pan over medium high heat. Lift edges frequently to allow uncooked portion to flow underneath. Sprinkle 1/4-1/2 cup cheese over center portion of omelette. Cover and cook 1-2 minutes over medium heat. Add 1/2 cup seafood mixture on top of one half of omelette. Cover and cook until egg mixture is set (approx. 2 minutes). Fold omelette over seafood portion and slide omelette onto a warm plate. Garnish top with halved shrimp and a sprig of parsley. Serve with fresh fruit and hot muffins. Makes 4 (2 egg) omelettes. You can also make one egg omelettes and reduce filling accordingly.

*Carol's Corner
The combination of flavors is perfect! An impressive dish!

Lost Canyon Lake Lodge

Innkeepers Beth Newman, an intensive care nurse, and Ken Nickson, an emergency department physician, welcome guests to Lost Canyon Lake Lodge. The warm and inviting common room features a moss rock fireplace and lots of wood and glass.

Area activities and events guests enjoy include water-skiing, canoeing, houseboating, windsailing, horseback riding, hiking, skiing, square dancing, concerts in the park, chuckwagon dinners and gold panning.

INNKEEPERS:	*Beth Newman & Ken Nickson*
ADDRESS:	*PO Box 1289*
	Dolores, CO 81323
TELEPHONE:	*(970) 882-4913; (800) 992-1098*
ROOMS:	*4 Rooms; Private baths*
OPEN:	*Year-round*
CHILDREN:	*Welcome*
ANIMALS:	*Prohibited*
SMOKING:	*Permitted outside only*

Mexican Eggs

8 oz. cottage cheese
5 eggs, slightly beaten
1 (4 oz.) can green chilies, drained
2 c. Monterey Jack cheese, shredded
2 T. flour
2 T. margarine, melted
1/2 t. baking powder

Combine all ingredients. Pour into a 9-inch pie plate that has been generously sprayed with cooking spray. Bake at 400° F. for 10 minutes. <u>Reduce</u> oven temperature to 350° and continue baking for 20 minutes more or until center is set. Serve with sour cream and mild salsa. Serves 4.

Note: This recipe can be doubled and baked in a 9x13-inch baking dish. It will then serve 8-10.

Open Box H

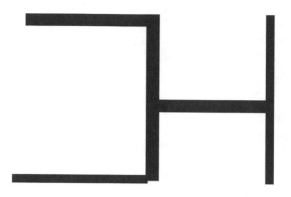

The Open Box H Bed and Breakfast was completed in 1989. The new design includes passive solar heating with large high windows that showcase the spectacular mountain views. In winter, the Frisco Flyer bus stops at the front door. It connects with the Summit Stage bus. With this combination, guests go almost any place in Summit County - FREE!

The brand, OPEN BOX H, has been a part of the Hugins heritage since the 1890's.

INNKEEPERS: *Chuck & Phyllis Hugins*
ADDRESS: *711 Belford; PO Box 1210*
Frisco, CO 80443
TELEPHONE: *(970) 668-0661*
ROOMS: *2 Rooms; 2 Suites; All with private baths*
OPEN: *Year-round*
CHILDREN: *Welcome*
ANIMALS: *Prohibited*
SMOKING: *Prohibited*

Corned Beef Hash and Eggs

1 can (15 oz.) corned beef hash, chilled
4 eggs
4 slices of bread, toasted
Cheddar cheese, finely shredded (optional)

Remove both ends of chilled can. Push hash out and slice into 4 patties. Brown patties on each side in a skillet. Make a slight indentation in the hash and break an egg on each patty. Cover each egg with a small baking cup or cover the pan with a lid and cook until eggs are set. Top with a little cheese, if desired. Serve on a slice of toast. Makes 4 servings.

Scrubby Oaks

Guests enjoy spectacular sunrises and sunsets at Scrubby Oaks Bed and Breakfast. The vista is unexcelled! The antiques, art works, books and pictures inside the inn showcase the Craig family history. Guests delight in gourmet country breakfasts, which vary each morning.

In February 1995, an article about Scrubby Oaks was published in the Sunday travel section of the *Atlanta Journal.*

INNKEEPERS:	*Mary Ann Craig*
ADDRESS:	*1901 Florida Road; PO Box 1047*
	Durango, CO 81302
TELEPHONE:	*(970) 247-2176*
ROOMS:	*7 Rooms; Private and shared baths*
OPEN:	*Last weekend in April through October*
CHILDREN:	*Welcome*
ANIMALS:	*Prohibited*
SMOKING:	*Prohibited*

Huevos Rancheros

Serve with homemade sopapillas!

4 flour tortillas
1 lb. sausage
1 (10 oz.) can enchilada sauce
Onion, chopped
Yellow cheese, grated
4 eggs, fried
Lettuce, chopped
Guacamole

> **⚘ Carol's Corner**
> *To save time, buy prepared tortilla "bowls." For lower fat intake, instead of deep fat frying, warm the flour tortillas in microwave and place flat on serving plate. Pile rest of ingredients on top, using a poached egg.*

Day before serving, deep fat fry flour tortillas in a tortilla basket, which shapes them into attractive serving bowls. In the morning, put the tortilla baskets in the oven on WARM. Cook, drain and crumble the sausage. Mix it with the enchilada sauce and heat thoroughly. Fry eggs.

Layer in this order in tortilla bowls:
    Enchilada-sausage mixture
    Onion
    Cheese
    Fried egg
    More cheese
    Lettuce
    Guacamole   Serves 4.

Homemade Sopapillas

Thaw frozen bread dough (or make your own) and break off small pieces. Roll very thin and drop into hot oil in a deep fat fryer. Turn as soon as bottom side is golden, and fry on other side. They will puff up. Drain on paper towels. Serve with honey, jam and butter.

Hughes Hacienda

The comfort and spaciousness of Hughes Hacienda make it the ideal get-away. The decor (complete with beamed ceilings, Mexican tile, and a kiva-style fireplace) casts a spell on the guests of the Hacienda.

The Hacienda has one suite that is furnished with a fireplace, sitting area with library, stereo, TV, wet bar, refrigerator and microwave oven. A full gourmet breakfast is served each morning in the privacy of the suite or on the portal overlooking the mountains and valley.

INNKEEPERS:	*Wayne & Carol Hughes*
ADDRESS:	*12060 Calle Corvo*
	Colorado Springs, CO 80926
TELEPHONE:	*(719) 576-2060*
ROOMS:	*1 Suite; Private bath*
OPEN:	*Year-round*
CHILDREN:	*Prohibited*
ANIMALS:	*Prohibited*
SMOKING:	*Prohibited*

Breakfast Enchiladas

2 T. butter
1 heaping T. flour
3/4 c. chicken broth
1/2 c. milk
Salt and pepper, to taste
1 serrano chile pepper, minced very fine (remove seeds)
2 eggs
1/4 c. zucchini, chopped
1/4 c. tomato
1 T. pepitas (pumpkin seeds)
2 corn tortillas
1/2 c. Farmers cheese, grated
4 slices avocado, for garnish

Make a white sauce by melting the butter over medium heat. Stir in the flour to form a paste. Add the chicken broth, milk, salt and pepper. Stir constantly until it bubbles and thickens. Stir in the serranos and simmer on low heat while preparing the rest of the dish. Scramble the eggs with the diced zucchini, tomato and pumpkin seeds. Pat the tortillas with wet hands to moisten and place on a preheated hot grill or skillet, turning after 30 seconds. Heat on the second side 30-40 seconds. Place the tortillas on a serving plate and spoon the cooked egg mixture down the center of each tortilla, rolling the tortillas around the eggs and rotating so the seam side is down. Pour the sauce over the enchiladas and sprinkle with cheese. Garnish with the avocado slices. This can be served with an assortment of fresh fruit, a meat, hashbrown potatoes or pinto beans.

> **Carol's Corner**
> *Farmers cheese is a soft, very mild white cheese. Wonderful delicate flavor! Most supermarkets have it available in the deli section. If you are unable to find it, substitute with Monterey Jack or Havarti. Wayne Hughes, owner and chef at Hughes Hacienda, has quite a flair when it comes to Mexican food. His combination of taste, texture and color is sensational.*

Ellen's

Ellen's
Bed
&
Breakfast

Veteran travelers and those with dreams of faraway places will enjoy visiting with innkeepers Baldwin "Baldy" and Ellen Ranson at their homestay in Longmont. The Ransons lived for several years in both Korea and Japan where he taught economics through the University of Maryland and she taught English.

The Ransons often host newlyweds who arrive in "decorated" cars. During breakfast, they watch Innkeeper "Baldy" out in the yard washing their cars as an added amenity!

INNKEEPERS:	*Baldwin & Ellen Ranson*
ADDRESS:	*700 Kimbark Street*
	Longmont, CO 80501
TELEPHONE:	*(303) 776-1676*
ROOMS:	*1 Room; Private bath*
OPEN:	*Year-round*
CHILDREN:	*Welcome*
ANIMALS:	*Permitted; Resident pets*
SMOKING:	*Permitted*

Fluffy Stuffers

Bakery croissants
Eggs
Butter
Swiss cheese, sliced thin
Turkey, sliced thin
Fresh asparagus spears (parboil 1 minute)
Hollandaise sauce (can use Knorr's mix)
Dash cayenne pepper

For each guest, slice one croissant in half lengthwise. Wrap in foil and warm in low oven. Soft scramble eggs in butter. Open croissant and on bottom half gently stuff with egg, a slice of cheese and a slice of turkey. Crisscross 2 asparagus spears on top. Put the top half on to close the croissant. Return "package" to oven for a few minutes to melt cheese. Place on heated plates. Pour hot Hollandaise sauce over top. Sprinkle with a dash of cayenne to give it some zing! Add a side of 2 or 3 sliced fresh fruits.

Carol's Corner

I agree with Ellen at Ellen's Bed and Breakfast when she says, "Impressive presentation, easy preparation." The amount of the ingredients will vary depending on individual tastes and number of guests. For variety, try using ham, or leave the meat out altogether and use several different vegetables to please your vegetarian friends.

Meadow Creek

ASABATTLES

Hosts Pat and Dennis live in a log cabin adjacent to Meadow Creek Bed and Breakfast. Hosts Judy and Don (Pat and Judy are sisters) live in Littleton but can be found most Saturdays and alternate Sundays at the inn. The two barns, smoke house, gift cabin and other structures are all listed in the Colorado Historical Register.

Within a short driving distance are hiking and biking trails, fishing, horses, cross-country skiing and small towns to visit.

INNKEEPERS:	*Pat & Dennis Carnahan; Judy & Don Otis*
ADDRESS:	*13438 US Highway 285*
	Pine, CO 80470
TELEPHONE:	*(303) 838-4167; (303) 838-4899*
ROOMS:	*5 Rooms; 2 Suites; All with private baths*
OPEN:	*Year-round*
CHILDREN:	*Discouraged; Not child-proof*
ANIMALS:	*Prohibited*
SMOKING:	*Outside only*

Ham Quiche Biscuit Cups

1 (8 oz.) pkg. cream cheese, softened
2 T. milk
2 eggs
1/2 c. Swiss cheese, shredded
2 T. green onion, chopped
1 can (10 count) refrigerated flaky biscuits
1/2 c. ham, finely chopped

Preheat oven to 375° F. Grease 10 muffin cups. Beat cream cheese, milk and eggs until smooth. Stir in Swiss cheese and green onions. Separate dough into 10 biscuits. Place one biscuit in each cup. Firmly press in bottom and up sides, forming a 1/4-inch rim. Place half of ham in bottom of dough cups. Spoon about 2 tablespoons cheese and egg mixture over ham. Top with remaining ham and bake for about 25 minutes or until filling is set and edges of biscuits are golden brown. Remove from pan. Serve immediately. Serves 10.

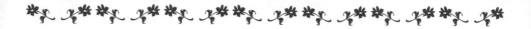

Our Hearts Inn

Our Hearts Inn, located in Old Colorado City, is a 100-year-old inn with arches and curved ceilings on the first floor. Cowboy and western stenciling, antiques, hearts, bunnies and rocking chairs (no room is complete without one) give a nostalgic glimpse of the past.

Guests are encouraged to stroll the tree-lined streets of antique and boutique shops in Old Colorado City, the restored historic district of Colorado Springs.

INNKEEPERS:	*Andy & Pat Fejedelem*
ADDRESS:	*2215 W. Colorado Avenue*
	Colorado Springs, CO 80904
TELEPHONE:	*(719) 473-8684; (800) 533-7095*
ROOMS:	*3 Rooms; All with private baths; 1 Cottage*
OPEN:	*Year-round*
CHILDREN:	*Children over 12 are welcome*
ANIMALS:	*Prohibited*
SMOKING:	*Prohibited*

Summer's Bounty Zucchini Pie

1 egg, beaten
1/4 c. green onion, finely chopped (optional)
1/4 c. Parmesan cheese, grated
3 c. hash brown potatoes, refrigerated loose pack

In a large bowl, combine the egg, green onion and Parmesan cheese. Stir in potatoes. Transfer potato mixture into a 9-inch pie plate or quiche pan. Pat the mixture into the bottom and up the sides of the pan. Bake uncovered in a 400° F. oven for 35-40 minutes. Cool slightly (or refrigerate overnight).

2 T. olive oil
2 1/2 c. zucchini, thinly sliced (about 2 medium)
3 eggs, beaten
1/2 c. milk
1/4 t. salt
1/4 t. pepper
1/8 t. nutmeg
1/8 t. parsley
Oregano, to taste
1 1/2 c. mozzarella cheese

Heat olive oil in a large skillet. Cook zucchini until crisp and tender; cool slightly, then arrange over potato crust. In a small mixing bowl, combine the eggs, milk and spices. Stir in mozzarella cheese and pour atop the zucchini mixture in the crust. Bake in a 350° F. oven for 25-30 minutes or until filling appears set. Let stand for 10 minutes before serving. Great served with sliced tomatoes or baked tomatoes.

Outlook Lodge

Built in 1889 as a parsonage for a neighboring church, the lodge has hosted many guests since the early 1950's. Guests enjoy hiking, sightseeing in the Pike's Peak area, skiing at local resorts, horseback riding or just marveling at the natural sandstone formations in the Garden of the Gods.

The Outlook Lodge Bed and Breakfast is ideally suited for conferences, weddings, reunions, receptions or workshops.

INNKEEPERS:	*Hayley, Pat & Taylor Moran*
ADDRESS:	*PO Box 5*
	Green Mountain Falls, CO 80819-0005
TELEPHONE:	*(719) 684-2303*
ROOMS:	*4 Rooms; Each with private bath*
OPEN:	*Year-round*
CHILDREN:	*Welcome*
ANIMALS:	*Prohibited*
SMOKING:	*Prohibited*

Ham Strata

12 slices (regular size) white bread
12 oz. cheddar cheese, shredded (or Old English cheese slices)
10 oz. pkg. frozen chopped broccoli (thawed)
2 c. cooked ham, chopped or thin slices
6 eggs
2 1/2 c. milk
2 T. instant onion
1/2 t. salt
1/4 t. dry mustard
Cheddar cheese, shredded, for garnish, last 5 minutes of baking time

Cut 12 round shapes from bread using a cookie cutter or top of glass, approximately 3-inches in diameter. Set aside the round shapes. Tear the scraps into bite-size pieces and place in bottom of a 9x13-inch baking dish prepared with cooking spray. Arrange cheese on top of bread scraps. Add a layer of broccoli and then a layer of ham. Place bread circles on top – arrange in 3 rows of 4 bread circles each. Combine remaining ingredients (except cheese for garnish) and pour over ingredients in the pan, including bread circles. Cover and refrigerate overnight, or at least for 6-8 hours. Bake uncovered at 325° F. for approximately 60-65 minutes. Sprinkle with some cheddar cheese last 5 minutes and continue to bake until cheese melts. Let stand at least 5 minutes before cutting.

Raindrop

Raindrop Bed and Breakfast would like to give thanks

for all the ways our patrons allow us to grow and be!

L ocated on twenty-six acres at the mouth of the Poudre Canyon, Raindrop Bed and Breakfast offers privacy and tranquility in the rolling foothills of the Rocky Mountains. Sports enthusiasts enjoy biking, hiking, fishing, skiing or river rafting.

Guests of the Raindrop Bed and Breakfast experience "a retreat in nature".

INNKEEPERS:	*Tara Parr*
ADDRESS:	*6901 McMurry*
	Bellvue, CO 80512
TELEPHONE:	*(970) 493-0799*
ROOMS:	*3 Rooms; Private and shared baths*
OPEN:	*Year-round*
CHILDREN:	*Welcome*
ANIMALS:	*Prohibited*
SMOKING:	*Prohibited*

Chili Rellenos Casserole

1 c. tofu, crumbled
1 c. Monterey Jack cheese, grated
1/3 c. olives (any kind)
12 Poblano chilies, roasted, or use Anaheim for milder taste (can be purchased fresh roasted at farmers' market and frozen until needed)
4 eggs, separated
3 T. butter, melted
Sour cream
Salsa

Mix tofu, cheese and olives together for filling. Set aside. Remove skins and seeds from roasted chilies. Fill chilies with tofu mixture and lay in a buttered 8x11-inch (or similar size) casserole dish. Beat egg yolks well and add melted butter. In a separate bowl, beat egg whites until stiff and fold into egg yolk mixture. Pour over chilies. Bake at 350° F. for about 40-45 minutes or until egg mixture is set. Top with sour cream and warm salsa. Serve with rice and beans.

"This is a very hearty dish! All of our eggs are from our free range chickens. Our guests see the chickens walk by while they eat breakfast. I love to garden and cook and I use mainly organic ingredients and home grown veggies."
Tara Parr – Raindrop B&B

Romantic RiverSong Inn

R omantic River Song is a small mountain country inn nestled at the
foot of Giant Track Mountain in Estes Park. Its past history includes
Great Gatsby-like parties. Once a luxurious summer home of the
wealthy, River Song is now a very special and inviting bed and breakfast
inn.

Located at the end of a country lane on twenty-seven wooded acres,
guests enjoy the breathtaking panorama of snow-capped peaks in adjacent
Rocky Mountain National Park.

INNKEEPERS:	*Gary & Sue Mansfield*
ADDRESS:	*PO Box 1910*
	Estes Park, CO 80517
TELEPHONE:	*(970) 586-4666*
ROOMS:	*9 Rooms; All with private baths*
OPEN:	*Year-round*
CHILDREN:	*Not suitable for children*
ANIMALS:	*Prohibited*
SMOKING:	*Outside only!*

Chipotle Pico de Gallo Pie

1 c. Monterey Jack cheese, shredded
2 T. flour
1 c. chipotle pico de gallo, drained, divided (recipe below)
1/2 c. half and half
1/4 c. red bell pepper, chopped
1/4 c. green bell pepper, chopped
3 eggs, slightly beaten
1/4 t. salt
1/2 t. coarse ground black pepper
Prepared 9-inch pie crust, unbaked (do not use "deep dish")
1 small tomato, chopped

Toss cheese with flour. Add 1/3 cup pico de gallo, half and half, red pepper, green pepper and eggs. Add salt and pepper. Pour into pie crust and bake at 350° F. for 35-40 minutes or until set. Heat remaining 2/3 cup pico de gallo with chopped tomato. Serve over pie. This recipe is featured on the cover.

<u>Chipotle Pico de Gallo</u>
4 chipotle peppers, soaked in hot water, seeds removed, finely
  chopped
Juice of 2 limes
2 cloves garlic, minced
1 bunch green onions, chopped
1 bunch fresh cilantro, chopped
2 lbs. tomatoes, chopped

Mix all ingredients together. Let stand at room temperature for 1 hour, stirring occasionally. Chill before serving. Makes 3 cups.

Stonehaven

S tonehaven Bed and Breakfast is a 1906 Victorian home that
has been restored to its original glory. The gazebo is an ideal place
for weddings, reunions or other gatherings for special occasions. For
events with 30 to 125 people, the entire house must be rented for at least
the night of the event.

The view of the Colorado National Monument from the Grey Room on
the second floor is breathtaking. It's a favorite room for anniversaries.

INNKEEPERS:	*Amy Kadrmas & Vance Morris*
ADDRESS:	*798 North Mesa Street*
	Fruita, CO 81521
TELEPHONE:	*(970) 858-0898; (800) 303-0898*
ROOMS:	*3 Rooms; 1 Suite; Private & shared baths*
OPEN:	*Year-round*
CHILDREN:	*Well-behaved children welcome*
ANIMALS:	*Prohibited; Local kennel can board pets*
SMOKING:	*Outside only*

Breakfast Dish

1 (32 oz.) bag O'Brien potatoes or hash browns (O'Brien potatoes
   have peppers and onions)
Breakfast meat of choice (ham, bacon, sausage, Canadian bacon)
6-8 eggs
Salsa supreme or taco sauce
Cheddar cheese, grated or sliced

Fry potatoes in a skillet until done, following package directions. While potatoes are frying, cook meat. Cook eggs over-easy. Assemble in an oiled 9x13-inch casserole dish in this order: Potatoes, salsa or taco sauce (amount determined by how hot you desire), meat, eggs and cheese. Bake at 350° F. for 5-10 minutes or until cheese melts. Serves 6-8. Very filling.

Carol's Corner
A hearty meal...perfect for big appetites. A great meal to serve guests before sending them out for a day on the slopes! The amount of each ingredient can vary depending on how many people you are serving and your own individual taste.

FRUIT
SPECIALTIES

Valley View

L ou and Jan Purin, owners and operators of the Valley View
Bed and Breakfast, were enthralled by their first encounter with
Colorado's Western Slope and its panoramic vistas of the world's largest
mesa. They decided to build a luxury bed and breakfast there so others
could share the same experience.

Valley View was meticulously hand-crafted by the Purin's to insure the
proper blend between modern amenities and old-fashioned quality.

INNKEEPERS: *Lou & Jan Purin*
ADDRESS: *888 21 Road*
Fruita, CO 81521
TELEPHONE: *(970) 858-9503*
ROOMS: *3 Rooms; Shared and private baths*
OPEN: *Year-round*
CHILDREN: *Children over 10 are welcome*
ANIMALS: *Dogs permitted outside; Can board horses*
SMOKING: *Outside only*

Four-Fruit Compote

1 (20 oz.) can pineapple chunks
1/2 c. sugar
2 T. cornstarch
1/3 c. orange juice
1 T. lemon juice
1 (11 oz.) can mandarin oranges, drained
3-4 unpeeled apples, chopped
2-3 bananas, sliced

Drain pineapple, reserving 3/4 cup juice. In a saucepan, combine sugar and cornstarch. Add pineapple juice, orange juice and lemon juice. Cook and stir over medium heat until thickened and bubbly; cook and stir 1 minute longer. Remove from heat; set aside. In a bowl, combine pineapple chunks, oranges, apples and bananas. Pour warm sauce over the fruit; stir gently to coat. Cover and refrigerate. Serves 12-16.

Carol's Corner
Refreshing! This citrus glaze is a wonderful complement to the medley of fruits. It would also be great to use fresh fruits when in season. Braeburn apples are especially wonderful for this recipe...crunchy!

Silver Wood

Silver Wood Bed and Breakfast is a contemporary home set in rural Colorado near Divide, where hiking and snowshoeing trails abound. Lake and stream fishing are easily available for the serious or recreational fisherman.

The Heritage Room offers a special experience for the Silver Wood guest. Select furnishings include a radio from the 1940's, a chest of drawers from the late 1920's and a hand-sewn quilt hanging.

INNKEEPERS:	*Larry & Bess Oliver*
ADDRESS:	*463 County Road 512*
	Divide, CO 80814
TELEPHONE:	*(719) 687-6784; (800) 753-5592*
ROOMS:	*2 Rooms; Both with private baths*
OPEN:	*Year-round*
CHILDREN:	*Children are welcome*
ANIMALS:	*Prohibited*
SMOKING:	*Prohibited*

Larry's Broiled Grapefruit

1/2 grapefruit per person
Pure maple syrup, about 1 T. per person
Maraschino cherries, 1 per person for garnish

Cut grapefruit in half, crosswise. With a serrated knife, cut out the core, then cut between sections and around the outside edge. Place on foil lined baking pan (one with 1/2-inch edge works best). Fill all empty space in grapefruit halves with maple syrup. Broil about 10 minutes, or until the tops bubble and turn brown. A few black spots are acceptable. Garnish with a maraschino cherry in the center. Serve warm on a salad plate with a grapefruit spoon.

Black Dog Inn

The Black Dog Inn Bed and Breakfast features four guest rooms which are named for the mountain peaks around Estes Park. Each room has been tastefully decorated with family antiques, uniting the charm of yesteryear with the comforts of today.

Guests relax in the new Snowdrift Peak suite with its antique queen-size bed, private bath with an oversized marble shower and a cozy sitting room and private library.

INNKEEPERS:	*Pete & Jane Princehorn*
ADDRESS:	*650 S. St. Vrain Avenue; PO Box 4659*
	Estes Park, CO 80517
TELEPHONE:	*(970) 586-0374*
ROOMS:	*4 Rooms; All with private baths*
OPEN:	*Year-round*
CHILDREN:	*Children welcome over the age of 12*
ANIMALS:	*Prohibited; Resident dog*
SMOKING:	*Prohibited*

Baked Grapefruit for Two

1 ruby red grapefruit
2 t. cinnamon-sugar mixture (or use honey and cinnamon), per half
Fresh fruit or mint leaf, for garnish

Slice grapefruit in half. Cut between and loosen grapefruit sections. Sprinkle grapefruit with cinnamon-sugar mixture. Place in oven on LOW (200-300°) and bake grapefruit until warm. The grapefruit can be left in the oven for as long as an hour. Remove from oven and place each half in a pretty bowl and garnish with fresh fruit or a mint leaf.

The Boulder Victoria

D.SPRINGER '90

One of Boulder's grandest original homes, The Boulder Victoria is a historic 1870's landmark that has been meticulously renovated. The recipient of Historic Boulder's Preservation Award and the City of Boulder's Landscape Design Award, it has been featured in *Country Living* magazine and *Bon Appetit* magazine.

Guests delight in afternoon tea, served with scones, lemon curd, shortbread and cakes. Evening port in the parlor provides a soothing conclusion to the day's activities.

INNKEEPERS:	*Zoe Kircos*
ADDRESS:	*1305 Pine Street*
	Boulder, CO 80302
TELEPHONE:	*(303) 938-1300*
ROOMS:	*6 Rooms; 1 Suite; All with private baths*
OPEN:	*Year-round*
CHILDREN:	*Unable to accommodate children under 12*
ANIMALS:	*Prohibited*
SMOKING:	*Prohibited*

The Victoria's Spiced Fruit Compote

Spice Bag
20 black peppercorns
12 allspice berries
12 whole cloves
1-inch piece fresh ginger, sliced
1 strip of lemon peel
1 strip of orange peel

Place all ingredients in center of a cheesecloth square. Bring corners of cheesecloth together and tie with string to form a small bag or parcel. Set aside while preparing other compote ingredients.

Compote
1 1/2 c. Port or Madeira
4 c. water
1 t. vanilla
1/4 c. honey (optional)
1 c. dried pineapple
2 c. dried apricots
2 c. dried apples
1/2 c. prunes
5 cinnamon sticks

Combine all ingredients, with spice bag, in heavy saucepan. Simmer over low heat for 30 minutes, stirring occasionally. Remove cinnamon sticks and spice bag before serving. Serve warm with yogurt or whipped cream.

Make-ahead tip: May be stored in refrigerator for up to a week.

Frontier's Rest

While sitting in a large, well-worn rocking chair on the Victorian porch of Frontier's Rest Bed and Breakfast Inn, guests listen to a mountain creek and watch the sun set over Pikes Peak. Later they eat homemade cobbler, one of the inn's many complimentary desserts.

This historic home dates back to the turn-of-the-century. It has a guest kitchen, beverage and cookie bar, delectable breakfasts and is located within easy walking distance to local attractions.

INNKEEPERS:	*Jeanne Vrobel*
ADDRESS:	*341 Ruxton Avenue*
	Manitou Springs, CO 80829
TELEPHONE:	*(719) 685-0588; (800) 455-0588*
ROOMS:	*4 Rooms; All with private baths*
OPEN:	*Year-round*
CHILDREN:	*Children allowed on a space available basis*
ANIMALS:	*Prohibited*
SMOKING:	*Prohibited*

Wake-Up Fruit

1/2 c. soft-style cream cheese, fat free variety
1/2 c. vanilla yogurt
1 T. honey
1 small honeydew melon (or cantaloupe or a combination)
1 1/2 c. fresh raspberries

Slice and peel honeydew melon and arrange on dessert plates. In a small bowl or in a blender, whip together cream cheese, yogurt and honey until smooth. Do not overwhip or the mixture will become too thin. Drizzle or ladle the mixture across melon wedges. Top with raspberries.

Make-ahead tip: Cream cheese mixture can be made in advance and refrigerated until serving time.

Lightner Creek Inn

D. COULLEY

The Lightner Creek Inn, located on six pristine acres with a duck pond and stream, offers a casual, yet elegant, romantic escape. Guests enjoy the privacy of the Carriage House (a 700 square foot studio) or any of the other nine guest rooms that are furnished with down comforters and antique furniture.

In the winter, guests can enjoy Nordic or Alpine skiing, experience a dinner sleigh ride or simply sit by a cozy fire.

INNKEEPERS:	*Suzy & Stan Savage*
ADDRESS:	*999 C.R. 207*
	Durango, CO 81301
TELEPHONE:	*(970) 259-1226; (800) 268-9804*
ROOMS:	*10 Rooms; All with private baths*
OPEN:	*Year-round*
CHILDREN:	*Welcome*
ANIMALS:	*Prohibited*
SMOKING:	*Prohibited*

Rhonda's Rummy Starter

Pecans, finely chopped, for garnish
Unsalted butter
Bananas
Peaches
Brown sugar
Cinnamon
Lemon juice
Rum
Canned whipped cream
Romanoff Sauce (recipe below)

Roast the chopped nuts in oven. Set aside. Slice bananas lengthwise and peaches thinly. Melt a dab of butter in non-stick pan over medium heat. Lightly sauté the peaches and bananas on one side. Sprinkle with brown sugar and cinnamon. Turn fruit over and sprinkle again with brown sugar and cinnamon and a little lemon juice. Watch carefully to avoid overcooking. When slightly golden, add dashes of rum to pan and swirl pan around until rum evaporates. Place fruit slices on plate in a fan shape, and drizzle with Romanoff Sauce. Spray with dollop of whipped cream. Sprinkle with toasted pecans and brown sugar. Serve warm.

<u>Romanoff Sauce</u>
1 1/2 c. dairy sour cream
2 T. powdered sugar
2 T. brown sugar
1 T. rum
1 t. orange peel, finely shredded
1/2 t. ground cinnamon
1/4 t. ground nutmeg

In a small bowl, stir together all ingredients. Cover and refrigerate for up to 24 hours to let flavors blend. Makes about 1 1/2 cups.

The Mary Lawrence Inn

T he Mary Lawrence Bed and Breakfast Inn is an Italianate building with two floors and five distinctive rooms. This unique bed and breakfast, completely renovated in 1989, is alive with vivid colors, sponged and stenciled walls, antiques, quilts and collectibles.

A delicious breakfast is served each morning for the hearty appetite or a special offering for the lighter appetite is available. Special diets will be accommodated with advance notice.

INNKEEPERS: *Pat & Jim Kennedy*
ADDRESS: *601 North Taylor*
Gunnison, CO 81230
TELEPHONE: *(970) 641-3343*
ROOMS: *4 Rooms; 1 Suite; All with private baths*
OPEN: *Year-round*
CHILDREN: *Ages six and older are welcome*
ANIMALS: *Prohibited; Two resident cats*
SMOKING: *Prohibited*

Melon with Peach Salsa

3 ripe peaches
2 ripe tomatoes
1 T. lemon juice
3 green onions, sliced
1-2 mild fresh green chiles (Anaheim), chopped
2 T. fresh cilantro, chopped
1/4 c. olive oil
2 T. sherry vinegar
1 T. honey
1-2 ripe Rocky Ford cantaloupes or other melon, cut into wedges
Cilantro sprigs, for garnish

Peel peaches and tomatoes; chop coarsely. In a large bowl, combine the peaches and tomatoes with lemon juice. Add green onions, green chiles and cilantro and mix well. In a small bowl, whisk together the oil, vinegar and honey. Pour over fruit/vegetable mixture and stir well. Cover and refrigerate for at least 1 hour before serving. Makes 2 cups, approximately eight 1/4 cup servings.

To serve: Set one wedge of melon upright on a plate. Place salsa on melon. Garnish with cilantro sprig.

"In mid to late summer, Colorado produces the BEST cantaloupes and peaches. This recipe uses both in a unique and colorful way. We love to showcase these crops for our visitors."
Pat & Jim Kennedy – Mary Lawrence Inn

Sterling House

The Sterling House Bed and Breakfast home was built in 1886 on a quiet street in the heart of Greeley. When guests enter the front door, they are taken "back in time" to the ambiance of a bygone era. Sterling House is within walking distance of the University of Northern Colorado.

The Rose bedroom/sitting room suite is papered in rose tones. The bedroom includes a brass bed and feather comforter. The parlor has high ceilings, pocket doors and inviting furnishings.

INNKEEPERS: *Lillian Peeples*
ADDRESS: *818 12th Street*
  Greeley, CO 80631
TELEPHONE: *(970) 351-8805*
ROOMS: *2 Rooms; Both with private baths*
OPEN: *Year-round*
CHILDREN: *Children 10 and older permitted*
ANIMALS: *Prohibited*
SMOKING: *Permitted on enclosed porch*

Chocolate Covered Strawberries

1/2 c. chocolate chips
1 T. oil
12-14 strawberries
Optional: Chocolate sprinkles
Optional: White chocolate chips

Over a double boiler or in a microwave, melt chocolate chips until smooth. (Stir every 30 seconds until melted.) Add oil and mix well. Wash and dry strawberries. Hold them by their green stems and dip them into the chocolate mixture. Shake off excess. Roll in chocolate sprinkles, if desired. Lay on wax paper and refrigerate for one hour or until chocolate is firm. You can vary this recipe by using the white chocolate as well.

✳Carol's Corner

The Sterling House says, "For a light dessert, this recipe is easy and very romantic. It is also great for afternoon teas." I agree. My son Ryan and I had lots of fun experimenting with this recipe. We used several different fruits and used both kinds of chocolate and "double-dipped." Some favorites:

Strawberries *– dip in chocolate, then dip again (just the tip) in white chocolate.*

Golden delicious apples *– dip halfway in chocolate, then drizzle with white chocolate.*

Orange slices *– dip halfway in white chocolate, drizzle with chocolate.*

And ***almonds*** *– dip the pointed ends in the chocolate. Great!*

Two Sisters Inn

Two Sisters Inn is a gracious bed and breakfast that is nestled at the base of Pikes Peak. It mixes the charm of the past with the comfort of the present. Built in 1919 by two sisters as the Sunburst boarding house, it showcases an 1896 piano that is tucked into the parlor next to a red velvet fainting couch. An entire wall of cookbooks highlights the library.

"Can I just live here forever?"

~ Guest, Two Sisters Inn

INNKEEPERS:	*Wendy Goldstein & Sharon Smith*
ADDRESS:	*Ten Otoe Place*
	Manitou Springs, CO 80829
TELEPHONE:	*(719) 685-9684; (800) 2-SIS-INN*
ROOMS:	*4 Rooms; 1 Cottage; Private & shared baths*
OPEN:	*Year-round*
CHILDREN:	*Well-supervised children are welcome*
ANIMALS:	*Prohibited*
SMOKING:	*Prohibited*

Mango Melon Soup

1 small melon (your choice), peeled and cubed
1 ripe banana, peeled
1 mango, peeled and cubed (divided)
1 T. lemon juice
1 T. honey
Dash vanilla
6 mint leaves, for garnish
6 raspberries, for garnish

Place melon cubes in blender and process until smooth. Add banana, 1/4 cup mango cubes, lemon juice, honey and vanilla and blend until smooth. Chill mixture for several hours or overnight. Chill separately the remaining mango cubes. When ready to serve, divide mango cubes among six parfait cups. Stir chilled mixture and pour equally over the fruit. Garnish with raspberries and mint leaves. Makes 6 servings.

"Isn't it amazing how a culinary creation evolves? We needed a fruit course for a breakfast one morning and we searched the refrigerator for what was available. We came up with a ripe mango, some melon, and a banana and quickly whipped up all of these ingredients in a blender. We garnished it with some flowers from our flower and herb gardens and voila – a breakfast soup was born! We are resident schooled chefs preparing 'creative gourmet' breakfasts. We live to eat!"
Wendy Goldstein and Sharon Smith – Innkeepers at Two Sisters Inn

Romantic RiverSong Inn

R omantic RiverSong Bed and Breakfast Inn is located at the end of a
country lane on twenty-seven wooded acres that offers a rushing
trout stream, rustic gazebo and gentle hiking trails with rock benches.
Extra amenities available to guests include massages, candlelight gourmet
dinners, portable backpack picnic lunches and guided fly fishing
excursions.

Guests are lulled to sleep by the melody of a nearby mountain stream.

INNKEEPERS:	*Gary & Sue Mansfield*
ADDRESS:	*PO Box 1910*
	Estes Park, CO 80517
TELEPHONE:	*(970) 586-4666*
ROOMS:	*9 Rooms; All with private baths*
OPEN:	*Year-round*
CHILDREN:	*Not suitable for children*
ANIMALS:	*Prohibited*
SMOKING:	*Permitted outside only*

Banana Mango Smoothies

6 fresh ripe mangoes
Sugar, to taste
4 ripe bananas
2 (2 lb.) containers low fat vanilla yogurt

Peel and slice the mangoes. Place in a saucepan with water to cover and bring to boil. Cook until tender, about 20 minutes. Add small amounts of sugar, a little at a time, to sweeten, if they're too tart. Put mangoes into blender, reserving juice. Add bananas and yogurt. Blend until smooth, adding a little mango juice, if too thick. Chill. Stir and pour into serving glasses. Garnish with a strawberry on the rim of the glass for color. Makes 12-16 servings, depending on size of glass.

Carol's Corner

Tall glasses of Banana Mango Smoothies are featured on the cover. This is a healthy, cool and delightful drink for breakfast or a great "pick-me-up" for anytime throughout the day. Although the recipe makes a lot, it can easily be reduced to serve a smaller number of people. Be adventurous—use other fruits and create your own smoothies.

Eagle Cliff House

M ike and Nancy Conrin, owners of Eagle Cliff House, are backpacking and hiking consultants who are familiar with regulations and types of equipment. They gladly help guests plan treks into Rocky Mountain National Park for a day hike or an overnight back country experience.

Eagle Cliff House offers individualized services for birthdays, weddings, honeymoons, anniversaries or other special occasions.

INNKEEPERS:	*Nancy & Mike Conrin*
ADDRESS:	*2383 Highway 66; PO Box 4312*
	Estes Park, CO 80517
TELEPHONE:	*(970) 586-5425*
ROOMS:	*2 Rooms; 1 Cottage; All with private baths*
OPEN:	*Year-round*
CHILDREN:	*Welcome*
ANIMALS:	*Prohibited; Outdoor resident pets*
SMOKING:	*Prohibited*

Fruit Smoothies

2 or 3 bananas (ripe, overly ripe, or frozen)
1 can peaches, pears, or fruit cocktail (or any extra fresh ripe fruit)
1 c. orange juice
1 c. pineapple juice
1 box frozen strawberries or raspberries
Sugar or honey, to taste
1 scoop frozen vanilla yogurt, per serving

Put bananas, canned fruit, orange juice and pineapple juice in blender; blend
on high. Add frozen strawberries or raspberries and continue to blend until
you achieve desired consistency. Taste, and add sugar or honey, if desired.
Place scoop of frozen yogurt in a glass and pour smoothie mixture over it.
Serve with a spoon.

The Van Horn House

Located in Roaring Fork Valley, The Van Horn House at Lions Ridge Bed and Breakfast is within minutes of Aspen, Snowmass and Ski Sunlight ski areas. Nearby are the historic towns of Redstone, Marble and Glenwood Springs, home of the world famous hot springs pool.

Each of the four guest rooms has been furnished with antiques, lace curtains, stained glass and just plain charm and coziness!

INNKEEPERS: *John & Susan Laatsch*
ADDRESS: *0318 Lions Ridge Road*
Carbondale, CO 81623
TELEPHONE: *(970) 963-3605*
ROOMS: *4 Rooms; Two with private balconies*
OPEN: *Year-round*
CHILDREN: *Children over 8 are welcome*
ANIMALS: *Prohibited; Resident cat*
SMOKING: *Prohibited*

Honey-Poached Pears

3/4 c. orange juice
1/2 c. honey
2 T. lemon juice
Dash salt
4 fresh Bartlett pears
Unsweetened whipped cream
Cinnamon-sugar (optional)

Combine orange juice, honey, lemon juice and salt in saucepan. Heat. Peel, halve and core pears; cut into eighths. Add pear slices to honey mixture. Simmer gently 20 minutes, just until tender. Baste frequently during poaching. Cool in syrup. Spoon pear slices and some syrup into attractive serving dishes (stemmed glasses work well). Top with whipped cream and a dash of cinnamon-sugar, if desired. Serves 4.

"The syrup is rich and full of flavor – the honey dominates. This dish is best served at room temperature, although it can be served hot or cold as well."
Susan Laatsch – The Van Horn House at Lions Ridge

The Plover Inn

The Plover Inn Bed and Breakfast is located on the plains of northeastern Colorado. James Michener chose this area to symbolize the legendary West. Visitors may recognize the scenic background that was filmed for the television miniseries, *Centennial*.

Guests can observe more than 250 species of birds, including Colorado's state bird, the lark bunting, and the mountain plover for which The Plover Inn was named. A professional biologist provides birding tours, evening floodlight tours and guide service.

INNKEEPERS:	*Joyce Held*
ADDRESS:	*223 Chatoga Street; PO Box 179*
	Grover, CO 80729
TELEPHONE:	*(970) 895-2275*
ROOMS:	*4 Suites; Private and shared baths*
OPEN:	*Open May - October*
CHILDREN:	*Welcome*
ANIMALS:	*Prohibited*
SMOKING:	*Prohibited*

Rhubarb Sauce

4 c. chopped rhubarb
2 c. sugar
1/4 c. water
1 (8 oz.) pkg. raspberry or strawberry Jell-O
1 t. cinnamon

Combine rhubarb, sugar and water in saucepan and let sit for at least 30 minutes, stirring occasionally. Simmer over low heat 10 minutes for firm rhubarb pieces, or cook 20-30 minutes for a softer rhubarb. Add Jell-O and cinnamon. Stir to dissolve. Serve warm over pancakes, waffles or French toast.

Note: This recipe can be cut in half using a 3 oz. package of gelatin.

"I have an abundance of rhubarb plants, so in the spring and most of the summer, rhubarb is always on the menu. I use rhubarb in a lot of standard recipes such as muffins, coffee cakes, breads and sauces. This rhubarb sauce is a favorite over my roasted pancake."
Joyce Held – The Plover Inn B&B

SIDE DISHES

Crystal Inn

T he Crystal Inn Bed and Breakfast, located in historic Crested Butte, is filled with American antiques, including a working antique telephone. Each guest room in this quiet, but inviting inn is tastefully decorated with quilts, comforters and coordinated linen and window treatments.

Guests enjoy two living areas, fireplaces, television, indoor hot tub, great views, hearty country breakfasts and warm hospitality from owners Dennis and Charlene Goree.

INNKEEPERS:	*Dennis & Charlene Goree*
ADDRESS:	*624 Gothic Avenue; PO Box 125*
	Crested Butte, CO 81224
TELEPHONE:	*(970) 349-1338; (800) 390-1338*
ROOMS:	*5 Rooms; All with private baths*
OPEN:	*Year-round*
CHILDREN:	*Children 12 and older are welcome*
ANIMALS:	*Prohibited*
SMOKING:	*Prohibited*

Corn Casserole

2 cans (14 3/4 oz.) creamed corn
2 cans (15 1/4 oz.) whole corn, drained
1 medium onion, chopped and sautéed
1/2 c. butter, melted
4 t. sugar
Pepper, to taste
2 eggs, beaten
48 saltine crackers, crushed
8 oz. cheddar cheese, grated
1 jar (4 oz.) pimento, chopped
1 1/3 c. milk

Mix all ingredients together. Place in 9x13-inch casserole dish that has been sprayed with cooking spray. Bake at 350° F. for 45 minutes or until light brown and bubbly. Serves 12.

Make-ahead tip: This dish can be made in advance and refrigerated or frozen until ready to bake.

"This is just a great buffet or potluck dish to take to your next party. Everyone raves about it."
Charlene and Dennis Goree – Crystal Inn B&B

> **Carol's Corner**
> *I made this one day when I was in a hurry and didn't take the time to sauté the onion – it's great that way, too! An easy way to crush the crackers is in your hands as you're adding them to the bowl. This does not take long to prepare and yet it feeds a large group. Perfect for family holiday gatherings.*

Apple Orchard Inn

Owners John and Celeste Gardiner moved back to the United States in 1995 after having lived in Europe for six years. A few months later they purchased the Apple Orchard Inn Bed and Breakfast.

While living in Europe, Celeste took a course in general cuisine as well as pastry making at the Ritz-Escoffier Ecole de Gastronomie Francaise in Paris, France. She also studied "one-on-one" with Judy Witts Francini in Florence, Italy, where she learned Northern Italian cooking.

INNKEEPERS: *John & Celeste Gardiner*
ADDRESS: *7758 County Road 203*
Durango, CO 81301
TELEPHONE: *(970) 247-0751; (800) 426-0751*
ROOMS: *4 Rooms; 6 Cottages; All with private baths*
OPEN: *Year-round*
CHILDREN: *Children under 8 welcome in cottages*
ANIMALS: *Prohibited; Resident pets*
SMOKING: *Prohibited*

Rosemary Roasted Potatoes

About 2 lbs. new potatoes, cut into 1-inch cubes
3 T. olive oil
2 T. chopped fresh rosemary leaves
2 t. dried thyme
1 t. freshly ground black pepper
1 t. coarsely ground salt

Place potatoes in a large mixing bowl. Add the olive oil, herbs and spices and mix thoroughly. Spray a shallow roasting pan with cooking spray and spread potatoes in a single layer. Bake at 350° F. for about 45 minutes, stirring every 15 minutes or so. Bake until potatoes are browned on the outside and tender in the center. These are delicious for breakfast or for dinner with meat.

A serving suggestion: After baking the potatoes, add sautéed diced onion and green pepper. Place potato mixture in individual serving dishes and top with eggs (either fried, scrambled or poached) and sprinkle with cheddar cheese. Bake in a hot oven for a few minutes to melt cheese. Garnish with chopped chives and serve.

Engelmann Pines

Engelmann Pines Bed and Breakfast is a luxurious mountain home nestled among the pines with beautiful mountain views in the background. It is tastefully decorated with antique furnishings that create the charm found in a Victorian home.

The spacious guest area includes a TV room, large, comfortable sitting room with antique game table and a piano, full kitchen and a cozy reading room.

INNKEEPERS:	*Heinz & Margaret Engel*
ADDRESS:	*PO Box 1305*
	Winter Park, CO 80482
TELEPHONE:	*(970) 726-4632; (800) 992-9512*
ROOMS:	*7 Rooms; Private and shared baths*
OPEN:	*Year-round*
CHILDREN:	*Welcome*
ANIMALS:	*Prohibited*
SMOKING:	*Prohibited*

Gratin of Cheese and Potatoes

2 large cloves of garlic
6-8 large Idaho potatoes
2 c. grated Gruyere cheese
2 pints (4 c.) whipping cream
Salt, to taste
Freshly ground pepper, to taste

Preheat oven to 325° F. Rub bottom of 9x13-inch glass baking dish with garlic. Crush and chop garlic and put it in bottom of dish. Slice potatoes very thin and layer about 1/3 of them in bottom of dish. Sprinkle with salt and pepper and 1/3 of cheese. Pour 1/3 cream over all. Repeat layers 2 more times until all ingredients are used. Bake about 1 hour. Excellent for brunch with ham and scrambled eggs. Serve hot, but still tastes good cold. Serves 8.

Frontier's Rest

Tucked away at the back of Frontier's Rest Bed and Breakfast is the Belle Room. The window opens to a hundred-year-old stone terraced wall and a naturally forested hillside. Guests relax on a seven-foot Renaissance Revival queen-sized bed. A bath is attached, featuring an oval tub and shower combination and an authentic pedestal sink.

". . . to sleep in the treetops at the foot of the Rockies. Sounds like a dream. It happens here every night."

~ Owner, Jeanne Vrobel

INNKEEPERS:	*Jeanne Vrobel*
ADDRESS:	*341 Ruxton Avenue*
	Manitou Springs, CO 80829
TELEPHONE:	*(719) 685-0588; (800) 455-0588*
ROOMS:	*4 Rooms; All with private baths*
OPEN:	*Year-round*
CHILDREN:	*Children allowed on a space available basis*
ANIMALS:	*Prohibited*
SMOKING:	*Prohibited*

Frontier Potatoes

6-8 red potatoes (skins on)
3 strips bacon
1/2 red or orange pepper
2 T. butter
1 t. cumin seeds

Boil potatoes in a saucepan with water until tender. While potatoes are cooking, chop up bacon and slice the pepper julienne style (matchlike sticks). Drain potatoes when done and cut into chunky slices. Melt butter in a large skillet. Add bacon and red pepper and fry until pepper just starts to become tender. Add potatoes and cumin seeds. Cook until browned.

Carol's Corner
Pungent and savory, the whole cumin seeds give these potatoes a very distinctive flavor...a dish that would be welcome at breakfast, brunch or dinner.

The Gable House

The Gable House Bed and Breakfast is located on a picturesque, tree-lined street in the heart of historic Durango. Rooms are intimate and elegantly furnished with antiques, and each has a private entrance. Queen, double and single beds are available, as well as extra space if needed.

The Gable House is conveniently located five blocks from the Durango and Silverton Narrow Gauge Train Station and is just a few blocks from downtown Durango's delightful shops and restaurants.

INNKEEPERS: *Heather & Jeffrey Bryson*
ADDRESS: *805 E Fifth Avenue*
Durango, CO 81301
TELEPHONE: *(970) 247-4982*
ROOMS: *3 Rooms; Shared baths*
OPEN: *Year-round*
CHILDREN: *Children 10 and older welcome*
ANIMALS: *Prohibited*
SMOKING: *Smoking allowed on balconies only*

Heather's Pappas

6 large potatoes, parboiled (partially cooked)
4 T. butter
4 T. flour
4 c. chicken broth
2 T. dried green chile powder, mild (see comment below)
3/4 c. heavy cream
Salt and pepper, to taste
Canola oil
4 large eggs
1 c. cheddar cheese, grated
Chopped parsley, for garnish (optional)
Flour tortillas (optional)

Cook potatoes the night before and refrigerate. In the morning, make a roux: In a saucepan over medium heat, melt butter. Stir in flour and cook, stirring constantly, until mixture is smooth and bubbly. Pour in chicken broth and green chile powder. While stirring, bring to a boil. It will thicken somewhat, but will still have a souplike consistency. Blend in heavy cream, salt and pepper to taste. Fry potatoes in canola oil until brown. Fry or poach eggs. To assemble: Place 1/4 of potatoes in soup bowl, cover with 1/4 of green chile sauce. Sprinkle with cheddar cheese and place an egg on top. Garnish with chopped parsley and serve with warm tortillas on the side. Serves 4. Tip: Sauce can be prepared in advance and frozen.

> *"If you partied too much with your guests the night before and forgot to parboil the spuds, you can substitute toasted bagels topped with a slice of ham for the potatoes. Leftover sauce is good over pasta."*
> *Heather Bryson – Gable House*

Carol's Corner
Heather, at the Gable House, buys green chile powder at roadside stands on the highway between Albuquerque and her home in Durango. If you do not live in that area, the chile powder can be mail ordered. Call or write: Hatch Chile Express 622 Franklin P.O. Box 350 Hatch, New Mexico 87937 Tel. (505) 267-3226

The Lovelander

T he Lovelander Bed and Breakfast offers hearty gourmet breakfasts, summertime picnic lunches (guests keep the charming baskets as a memento of their visit), fax and copy service, concierge service, and tour or excursion planning.

The Lovelander Meeting and Reception Center is located directly across the street from the inn. It offers an elegant decor for meetings, weddings, receptions and private parties.

INNKEEPERS:	*Bob & Marilyn Wiltgen*
ADDRESS:	*217 West 4th Street*
	Loveland, CO 80537
TELEPHONE:	*(970) 669-0798; (800) 459-6694*
ROOMS:	*11 Rooms; All with private baths*
OPEN:	*Year-round*
CHILDREN:	*Children over the age of 10 are welcome*
ANIMALS:	*Prohibited*
SMOKING:	*Permitted on decks and porch*

Cheese and Pepper Grits with Zesty Tomato Sauce

1 1/2 c. instant grits
3 c. boiling water
2 garlic cloves
1 poblano chile pepper, seeded and sectioned
1 red bell pepper, seeded and sectioned
1/2 green bell pepper, seeded and sectioned
3/4 c. scallions, chopped
3/4 t. salt
1/4 t. fresh ground pepper
3/4 t. Tabasco sauce
6 T. butter, melted
2 eggs, beaten
1 1/2 c. sharp Cheddar cheese, shredded
3/4 c. Parmesan cheese, freshly grated
3 c. your favorite chunky salsa
3 Roma tomatoes, seeded and chopped, for garnish
Fresh cilantro leaves, for garnish

Cook grits in water to consistency of Cream of Wheat. Cool slightly. Combine garlic and peppers in food processor; pulse to a fine mince. In large bowl, combine grits and minced veggies. Add scallions, seasonings, butter and eggs. Mix well. Stir in cheeses. Spray individual ramekins or muffin cups with food release spray. Spoon grits mixture into container of choice, packing tightly. If using ramekins, place on a baking sheet. Bake at 350° F. for 30 minutes, or longer, until golden on top and completely set in the middle. To prepare the tomato sauce, pour salsa into a blender or food processor and puree until smooth. Pour puree through a fine strainer (pressing with the back of a spoon) to remove any remaining chunks. Pour into a saucepan and cook over medium heat to reduce until sauce is not watery. Cool and pour into a squeeze bottle. To serve, "paint" plates with sauce. Coarsely chop some cilantro leaves; sprinkle randomly on plate. Unmold grits and place on serving plate. Top with chopped tomato and garnish with a sprig of cilantro. Serves 8.

EVENING
ENTRÉES

The Outpost Inn

For many years Barbara and Ken Parker had been enjoying their visits to the Rocky Mountains. When they realized this experience was something they wanted to have on a permanent basis, they moved from New Jersey to Colorado. After a two-year search, they picked the Outpost Bed and Breakfast and Winter Park as their new residence.

"Come share the experience. Share the Rocky Mountains with us!"

~ Owners, Barbara and Ken Parker

INNKEEPERS:	*Barbara & Ken Parker*
ADDRESS:	*PO Box 41*
	Winter Park, CO 80482
TELEPHONE:	*(970) 726-5346; (800) 430-4538*
ROOMS:	*7 Rooms; All with private baths*
OPEN:	*Year-round*
CHILDREN:	*Welcome*
ANIMALS:	*Prohibited; Resident pets*
SMOKING:	*Prohibited*

Penne Provancale

1 large green bell pepper
1 large red bell pepper
1/2 large Spanish onion
1/4 c. olive oil
12-16 Roma tomatoes
1 can (12 oz.) butter beans, drained
1/4 c. fresh basil, coarsely chopped
1 lb. penne pasta

Slice the green and red peppers and onion into strips. Heat the olive oil in a skillet and sauté the vegetable strips until the onions are clear. Add the tomatoes; cover and simmer slowly on low for 20 minutes. Add drained beans and chopped basil. Cover and simmer 20 minutes more. Serve over penne pasta cooked al dente. Best when served immediately. Serves 6-8.

Carol's Corner

A beautiful blend of colors and flavors – a dinner sure to please your vegetarian friends! If you prefer your vegetables crisp-tender, shorten the simmer time. For a finishing touch, garnish with some chopped fresh parsley and finely shredded fresh Parmesan cheese.

Apple Orchard Inn

Owners John and Celeste Gardiner lived six years in Europe before moving back to the United States in 1995. While in Belgium, Celeste prepared the dessert for the restaurant in the American Women's Club of Brussels. She later taught cooking classes for the American women.

Each of the guest rooms and cottages is uniquely trimmed with exquisite hardwoods and features elegant furnishings.

INNKEEPERS:	*John & Celeste Gardiner*
ADDRESS:	*7758 County Road 203*
	Durango, CO 81301
TELEPHONE:	*(970) 247-0751; (800) 426-0751*
ROOMS:	*4 Rooms; 6 Cottages; All with private baths*
OPEN:	*Year-round*
CHILDREN:	*Children under 8 welcome in cottages*
ANIMALS:	*Prohibited; Resident pets*
SMOKING:	*Prohibited*

Chicken Breasts on
a Bed of Wild Mushrooms

2 c. chicken stock or broth
2 oz. dried mushrooms (cepes, morels, trompettes des mortes or a
   combination), thoroughly rinsed under running water and drained
1 lb. fresh cultivated mushrooms
6 T. unsalted butter
4 chicken breasts, boned and halved
1/2 c. finely chopped shallots
Freshly ground black pepper and salt, to taste
1 c. Port wine
1 c. heavy cream

Bring the chicken stock to a boil in a small saucepan. Pour it over the dried mushrooms in a small bowl. Let stand for at least 2 hours. Meanwhile, trim stems from fresh mushrooms. (Save stems for another purpose or discard.) Wipe mushroom caps with a damp paper towel and slice thin. Melt butter in skillet. Add chicken and brown lightly. Cover and simmer on low heat for about 15 minutes, turning chicken over half way through cooking time. Remove chicken breasts from pan and pour a little of melted butter over them and keep warm while preparing the sauce. Pour off all but about 2 tablespoons of fat and add the chopped shallots. Sauté gently for about 5 minutes without browning. Drain and coarsely chop the dried mushrooms, reserving the liquid. Add these dried mushrooms and the sliced fresh mushrooms to skillet and simmer for another 10 minutes. Stir occasionally and season with the pepper and salt, if needed. Add the reserved soaking liquid and wine to skillet and simmer for another 5 minutes, or until slightly thickened. Add the cream and simmer until the sauce is thick enough to coat a spoon. Place the chicken breasts on top of the mushroom sauce, cover and simmer for 5 minutes before serving.

"We have had wonderful success with our dinners and our guests really seem to enjoy the luxury of having dinner at the inn and then being able to retire to their rooms."
John and Celeste Gardiner – Apple Orchard Inn

Allenspark Lodge

S ince 1933, Allenspark Lodge has woven its special magic for the community and the weary traveler alike. Constructed of native stone and majestic ponderosa pine, its warmth and peacefulness have embraced and renewed its guests throughout the years.

A variety of snacks, hot soups, special desserts plus wine, beer and soft drinks are available in the Wilderquest Room. Box lunches are also available by advance request.

INNKEEPERS:	*Mike & Becky Osmun*
ADDRESS:	*PO Box 247*
	Allenspark, CO 80510
TELEPHONE:	*(303) 747-2552; (800) 206-2552*
ROOMS:	*13 Rooms; Private & shared baths; 3 Cabins; All with private baths*
OPEN:	*Year-round*
CHILDREN:	*Children 14 and older are welcome*
ANIMALS:	*Prohibited*
SMOKING:	*Prohibited*

Chicken Florentine Soup

Feeds a crowd!

3 cans (32 1/2 oz. size) chicken broth
2 c. water
8 chicken bouillon cubes
1 t. Accent (or salt to taste, if preferred)
2 T. pepper, coarse ground
1 t. marjoram
2 t. rosemary
2 c. red onions, sliced
2 c. carrots, sliced
1 large zucchini, chopped
1 c. celery, chopped
1 (12 oz.) pkg. multi-colored rotini pasta (spiral shaped)
1 c. cream sherry
12 pieces chicken thighs and breasts, pre-cooked

Heat chicken broth with water, bouillon cubes and spices. Add vegetables and simmer for 20 minutes, or until partially tender. Add pasta and cream sherry and boil for 8-10 minutes, or until pasta is done. Add cooked chicken to the pot for the last 5 minutes or so to heat through. Serves 26.

*"This is a healthy and fragrant soup, hearty enough for a meal!
Serve with homemade bread or crusty French rolls."*
Becky and Mike Osmun – Allenspark Lodge

Sky Valley Lodge

Warm weather activities at Sky Valley Lodge include hiking, biking, hot air balloon rides and rodeos. Winter guests enjoy downhill skiing and snowmobiling. For the cross-country skiing enthusiast, the famous ski trail, Devil's Hangover, ends at the lodge.

Complimentary gourmet continental breakfasts are served daily in the dining room or full breakfast and lighter-fare luncheon/dinner menus are available. A special "kiddy" nook provides diversions for children.

INNKEEPERS: *Jerry LaSage*
ADDRESS: *31490 East Highway 40; PO Box 3132*
Steamboat Springs, CO 80477
TELEPHONE: *(970) 879-7749; (800) 538-7519*
ROOMS: *24 Rooms; An entire lodge available for rental*
OPEN: *Year-round*
CHILDREN: *Welcome*
ANIMALS: *Allow small dogs in certain rooms*
SMOKING: *Prohibited*

Backyard B.Q. Soup

Use your grill to roast the vegetables for this soup!
3-4 heads (bulbs) of garlic
10 c. vegetable broth
1/2 c. tomato pesto
1 1/2 T. sugar
Salt and pepper, to taste
1 head cauliflower
1 eggplant
1 large onion
3 red peppers
10 plum tomatoes
3 ears corn

Bake garlic for 45 minutes at 350° F. (See note below.) Prepare soup stock: Heat vegetable broth with tomato pesto, sugar, salt and pepper. When garlic has finished baking, cool a bit, then squeeze garlic out of cloves and mash with fork. Add to stock. Cut cauliflower, eggplant, onion and peppers into large pieces. Cut tomatoes in half lengthwise. Grill vegetables until there are dark grill marks on all sides (but watch carefully so they don't burn). Cut up all grilled vegetables into bite-size pieces (cut corn from the ears) and put into stock.

Carol's Corner

If you have never tried baked garlic, you are in for a real treat! Be sure to bake some extra bulbs when trying the soup recipe, so that you have some left over to spread on French bread. When baked, garlic becomes very rich and mellow.

TO BAKE GARLIC: Peel some of the paperlike skin from around each bulb of garlic, leaving on just enough to hold the cloves together. Cut about 1/4-inch off the top of the bulbs to expose the garlic in the individual cloves. Place the bulbs, cut side up, on foil. Drizzle each bulb with 1 or 2 teaspoons of vegetable or olive oil. Sprinkle with a little salt and pepper, if desired. Fold the foil securely around the garlic. Place the foil packet in the oven at 350 degrees F. and bake about 45 minutes, or until the garlic is soft and tender. Cool slightly and gently squeeze the garlic out of the cloves. Spread on bread or use in recipes.

The Outpost Inn

Located on 40 acres facing the Continental Divide, The Outpost Bed and Breakfast Inn is a getaway for a weekend, week or more in the heart of one of Colorado's most beautiful and affordable resorts.

During ski season, guests of The Outpost enjoy free shuttle service to the ski areas of Winter Park and Mary Jane. For cross-country enthusiasts, Devil's Thumb and Idlewild trails are nearby.

INNKEEPERS:	*Barbara & Ken Parker*
ADDRESS:	*PO Box 41*
	Winter Park, CO 80482
TELEPHONE:	*(970) 726-5346; (800) 430-4538*
ROOMS:	*7 Rooms; All with private baths*
OPEN:	*Year-round*
CHILDREN:	*Welcome*
ANIMALS:	*Prohibited; Resident pets*
SMOKING:	*Prohibited*

Cilantro Chicken

1 lb. skinless, boneless chicken breasts
Cajun spice (hot)
Olive oil
1 large Spanish onion, diced coarse
1 large green bell pepper, diced coarse
8 Roma tomatoes, chopped
1 jar (16 oz.) mild picante sauce
1/4 c. cilantro, chopped

Cut chicken breasts into chunks and season with Cajun spice to taste. Heat olive oil in skillet and brown chicken. Add onions and peppers; sauté until onions are clear. Add tomatoes; cover and simmer for 15 minutes. Add picante sauce and cilantro. Cover and simmer <u>slowly</u> for 1 hour or until chicken is very tender. Serve with yellow rice and black beans. Serves 6.

Make-ahead tip: This dish can be prepared in advance and frozen.

"It has become my tradition to serve this low fat dish to celebrate Cinco de Mayo."
Barbara Parker – Outpost Inn

Carol's Corner

One afternoon I arrived home to be greeted by a delicious aroma. I asked Ryan and his friend Travis what smelled so good. Travis answered, "We found some chicken stuff in the refrigerator, put it in some pita bread, added a spoonful of sour cream and made ourselves a sandwich. It's <u>really</u> good – you should try it!" Well, that chicken stuff turned out to be the Cilantro Chicken I had made for dinner the night before. I'm sure the Parkers at Outpost Inn did not intend for it to be served in this way...but hey, why not?

Ellen's

The appeal of Ellen's Bed and Breakfast is the home-like atmosphere and good conversation. The one guest room has a queen-size, four-poster bed and a private bath that boasts an old-fashioned, bright green, footed bathtub. An additional small room with bunk beds accommodates two children.

Ellen sets her breakfast table with crystal and china and serves Eggs Benedict with asparagus, a three-cheese Santa Fe quiche or pecan waffles.

INNKEEPERS:	*Baldwin & Ellen Ranson*
ADDRESS:	*700 Kimbark Street*
	Longmont, CO 80501
TELEPHONE:	*(303) 776-1676*
ROOMS:	*1 Room; Private bath*
OPEN:	*Year-round*
CHILDREN:	*Welcome*
ANIMALS:	*Permitted; Resident pets*
SMOKING:	*Permitted*

Sweet & SauerKraut 'n Ribs

1 large can or bag (32 oz.) good brand sauerkraut
1/2 c. packed brown sugar (use more if you wish)
6 or 7 country style pork ribs (gotta be country style!)
1/2 red apple, unpeeled and finely diced

Empty kraut into a 9x13-inch glass baking dish that has been sprayed with cooking spray. Mix in about 1 cup of water and the brown sugar. Lay ribs on top. Cover fairly snugly with foil wrap. Bake s-l-o-w-l-y in a 325° F. oven all afternoon (about 4 hours). Then drain off some of the fatty liquid. Stir the red apple into the kraut for some color. Bake uncovered for another 1/2 hour. Serves 3 or 4.

"Serve this HOT with homemade
mashed potatoes. Super good stuff
for a winter day! Brown sugar is
the key! Freezes well."
Ellen Ranson – Ellen's B&B

⚜Carol's Corner
I am very fond of sauerkraut so this is one of my favorites! Try putting it in a crockpot (along with some onion slices and omitting the apple, for variety) before you go to work in the morning. You'll love having dinner ready when you arrive home.

Kelly Place

Built in the mid-1960's, the Kelly Place Bed and Breakfast Lodge is an adobe-style building with courtyards. It is located ten miles west of Cortez in McElmo Canyon, where over 25 Anasazi sites have been documented.

A full-time archaeologist is employed to teach archaeology classes and to oversee the excavation and restoration of the sites. The Lodge borders BLM (Bureau of Land Management) lands that have 6,000 acres of Anasazi sites and hiking trails.

INNKEEPERS:	*Kristie Carriker*
ADDRESS:	*14663 County Road G*
	Cortez, CO 81321
TELEPHONE:	*(970) 565-3125; (800) 745-4885*
ROOMS:	*8 Rooms; All with private baths*
OPEN:	*Year-round*
CHILDREN:	*No charge for children six and under*
ANIMALS:	*Prohibited; Resident pet*
SMOKING:	*Prohibited*

Kelly Place Beef and Beans

1 qt. (4 c.) dry pinto beans
2 qt. (8 c.) water
2 lb. pot roast
1 large onion, chopped
1 T. salt
1 c. catsup
1/2 c. dark molasses
2 T. mustard
1 t. liquid smoke
5 or 6 pieces <u>crystallized</u> ginger

Soak the beans overnight in the water. Next morning add the uncooked roast, onion and salt. Cook until meat is done, adding more water as necessary, but <u>not</u> so much as to make a great deal of broth. Remove the roast, debone and strip the beef into smaller pieces (bite-size). Return the beef to the beans and add remaining ingredients. Simmer at least 4 hours, the longer the better. And as with most beans...better the next day!

Carol's Corner
Want to eliminate the stress of cooking and kitchen clean-up when you are entertaining? Make this recipe a day in advance, or even several days or weeks in advance and freeze it. It can also be made in a crockpot.

Mt. Blanca Game Bird & Trout

Mt. Blanca Game Bird and Trout has something for everybody. 6,000 acres of private and secluded wooded lakes and lush meadows provide guests with the best in upland game and migratory bird hunting, trout fishing, sporting clays and hiking.

Reservations are required for accommodations, meals, bird hunts, sporting clays and fishing. A gift shop carries sundries, including clothing.

INNKEEPERS:	*Roger Wakasugi & Jerry Smith*
ADDRESS:	*PO Box 236*
	Blanca, CO 81123
TELEPHONE:	*(719) 379-DUCK*
ROOMS:	*8 Rooms; All with private baths*
OPEN:	*Year-round*
CHILDREN:	*Welcome*
ANIMALS:	*Outside only; Dog training and boarding*
SMOKING:	*Permitted*

Pheasant with Ham and Bacon

4 pheasant breasts, split and deboned
1 pkg. (8 slices) smoked ham
16 slices bacon
1 can cream of mushroom soup
1 carton (8 oz.) sour cream

Wash pheasant breasts; pat dry. Wrap 1 slice of ham around each breast. Then wrap 2 slices of bacon around ham. Place in a greased casserole dish. Combine mushroom soup and sour cream and pour over top of pheasant breasts. Bake covered at 150° F. for 2 hours, or until done and tender. Uncover last 20 minutes of baking time. Serving suggestion: Serve over wild rice, accompanied with Spiced Cranberries. Makes 8 servings.

<u>**Spiced Cranberries**</u>
1 lb. cranberries
2 c. sugar
2 T. white vinegar
1 T. cinnamon
Orange juice (amount is your preference)

Combine all ingredients in a saucepan, adding enough orange juice to moisten. Cook over low heat about 30 minutes. Serve warm.

Stonehaven

S tonehaven Bed and Breakfast is surrounded by some of the most beautiful views in Colorado. To the east of the inn is the Grand Mesa, the largest flat top mountain in the world. To the north of the inn are the bookcliffs. The Colorado National Monument is south of the inn. All of these attractions are within a short drive from Stonehaven.

Guests can order breakfast in bed or be served a special lunch or dinner in the gazebo.

INNKEEPERS:	*Amy Kadrmas & Vance Morris*
ADDRESS:	*798 North Mesa Street*
	Fruita, CO 81521
TELEPHONE:	*(970) 858-0898; (800) 303-0898*
ROOMS:	*3 Rooms; 1 Suite; Private and shared baths*
OPEN:	*Year-round*
CHILDREN:	*Well-behaved children are welcome*
ANIMALS:	*Prohibited; Local kennel can board pets*
SMOKING:	*Outside only*

Pasta with Shrimp Sauce

1/4 c. salad oil
2 c. sliced mushrooms
3/4 c. chopped onion
2 cloves garlic, minced
3/4 lb. medium shrimp, shelled and deveined (set aside 1/2 cup)
1 can (10 3/4 oz.) cream of mushroom or cream of shrimp soup
1/4 c. dry white wine
1/4 c. milk
1/4 lb. (about 1/2 c.) bay scallops or 1 can (6 1/2 oz.) minced clams
Pasta of choice
Chopped parsley, for garnish (optional)

Heat oil in skillet and sauté mushrooms, onion and garlic. Add shrimp (except for reserved 1/2 cup) and cook until just done (takes just a few minutes). Add soup, wine and milk. In a small skillet, sauté the scallops or clams with the reserved shrimp. Meanwhile, bring water in a pot to a boil and cook pasta. Try to time everything to be done at the same time; overcooking seafood will make it tough. To serve, place pasta on dinner plate and top with shrimp sauce. Top with a small amount of sautéed scallops or clams and shrimp. Garnish with chopped parsley.

West Pawnee Ranch

The West Pawnee Ranch Bed and Breakfast is a working ranch located on the peaceful prairie in northeastern Colorado. Guests can participate in ranch routines that include moving cattle, branding or calving. They may also ride along with the owner as they check cattle, fences and water wells.

The ranch is 20 miles from the nearest cafe, so the owners offer additional meals. After the evening meal, guests relax on the patio and enjoy the panoramic view of the prairie with the Chalk Bluffs in the background.

INNKEEPERS:	*Paul & Louanne Timm*
ADDRESS:	*29451 Weld County Road 130*
	Grover, CO 80729
TELEPHONE:	*(970) 895-2482*
ROOMS:	*2 Rooms; Both with private baths*
OPEN:	*Year-round*
CHILDREN:	*Children are always welcome!*
ANIMALS:	*Prohibited*
SMOKING:	*Prohibited*

Beef Kabobs

1/4 c. vegetable oil
2 T. Worcestershire sauce
1 T. chopped fresh thyme (or 1 1/2 t. dried)
1/4 t. salt
1/4 t. freshly ground black pepper
12 cubes (1 1/4-inch) boneless top sirloin beef (about 1 lb.)
1 large red pepper, cored, seeded, cut into 1 1/2-inch pieces
1 large green pepper, cored, seeded, cut into 1 1/2-inch pieces
2 ears fresh corn, each about 6" long, cut crosswise into 4 pieces
1 large onion, peeled but root end left intact, cut into 8 wedges
1 to 1 1/2 c. prepared barbecue sauce, optional
Fresh herb sprigs, optional

In large bowl using wire whisk or fork, mix together oil, Worcestershire sauce, thyme, salt and pepper. Add beef, red and green peppers, corn and onions; toss gently to coat with marinade. Refrigerate while you prepare grill. Start fire in grill, placing rack 6 inches above coals. When coals are medium hot, after about 15 minutes, divide beef chunks and vegetable pieces equally among four 12-inch metal skewers. Place skewers on hot grill; cook 10-12 minutes until beef is medium rare and vegetables are lightly browned and tender. Turn kabobs frequently during cooking, brushing, if desired, with barbecue sauce. If desired, serve garnished with fresh herbs and accompanied by additional barbecue sauce, heated. Makes 4 servings.

"This beef kabob recipe is a favorite. We can have the ingredients ready, and when we return from a horseback ride, it's easy to put together and serve."
Louanne Timm – West Pawnee Ranch

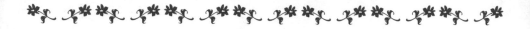

Conejos Ranch

For over 100 years, the Conejos Ranch has been the traveler's choice in south central Colorado. Noted for its western hospitality and charm, guests enjoy excellent accommodations and breathtaking scenery.

The Conejos River Ranch is nestled in the Rio Grande National Forest with a mile of Conejos River frontage and has been featured in *America's Wonderful Little Hotels and Inns.*

INNKEEPERS:	*Ms. Shorty Fry*
ADDRESS:	*25390 HWY 17*
	Antonito, CO 81120
TELEPHONE:	*(719) 376-2464*
ROOMS:	*8 Rooms; All with private baths; 6 Log Cabins*
OPEN:	*May-November; Calls taken year-round*
CHILDREN:	*Welcome*
ANIMALS:	*Welcome*
SMOKING:	*Allowed*

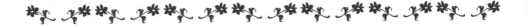

Conejos Ranch
Cornish Game Hens

2 Rock Cornish game hens
Salt
Pepper
Granulated garlic
1 or 2 apples
1/4 lb. (1 stick) butter
1 medium onion, diced
1/4 c. cream sherry

Preheat oven to 350° F. Wash hens and pat dry. Rub inside the hens with salt, pepper and granulated garlic. Dice the apples and stuff inside the hens. (If the hens are small, only one apple is needed.) Place hens breast side up on a rack in a roasting pan. Melt the butter in a skillet and sauté the onions with the cream sherry until the onions are clear. Put this mixture on top of the hens. Cover with foil or lid. Bake for 30-40 minutes; remove the cover and bake for 30 minutes more or until golden brown. Serves 2.

Carol's Corner
Remember to plan ahead for this recipe. Rock Cornish game hens usually come frozen, so allow thawing time in the refrigerator or microwave. Remove giblet package from thawed hen.

The Beulah House

The Beulah House Bed and Breakfast is located in the beautiful, scenic southwestern area of the Beulah Valley, 25 miles west of Pueblo. A six-acre back yard is bordered by locust and pine trees. One particular ponderosa pine stands 150 feet tall and is more than 200 years old.

The Sanctuary of St. Jude chapel is adjacent to the living room and can seat 45 people. The chapel has been the site of eight family baptisms and a family wedding.

INNKEEPERS:	*Harry & Ann Middelkamp*
ADDRESS:	*8733 Pine Drive*
	Beulah, CO 81023
TELEPHONE:	*(719) 485-3201*
ROOMS:	*3 Rooms; All with private baths*
OPEN:	*Summer*
CHILDREN:	*Welcome*
ANIMALS:	*Welcome; Resident pets*
SMOKING:	*Outside only*

Kibbe

2 1/2 lbs. fine ground lamb (or lean hamburger may be substituted)
1 large onion, grated
1/4 c. mint (or to taste), chopped
1 c. cracked wheat or bulgur (soaked for 10 minutes in 2 c. water)
1 stick of butter (not margarine), sliced (reserve for end of recipe)

Combine the raw meat, onion, mint and wheat (or bulgur). Put half of this mixture in the bottom of an 8x12-inch baking pan.

Stuffing Mix (middle layer)
1 lb. of meat (same type as above)
1 small onion, diced in small pieces
1/4 c. or more piñon (pine) nuts

Cook together the stuffing ingredients. Cool and put on top of raw mixture in baking pan. Use the remaining raw ingredients to cover stuffing mix. Score meat mixture into diamond shapes. Lay sliced butter on top. Bake at 350° F. for 1 hour or until butter disappears into meat. Serve with Lebanese Salad.

Lebanese Salad Dressing
1/2 c. vinegar or lemon juice
1/2 c. oil
2 cloves garlic
Mint to taste

"We owe these good dishes that our guests love to Nabeha Fidel Koury, a wonderful cook and a wonderful lady. I have noticed that our friends that have an Egyptian background make Kibbe as above, but with cinnamon and allspice also."
Ann Middelkamp – Beulah House

Combine ingredients by shaking in a jar. Refrigerate until ready to use. Just before serving, pour dressing over iceberg or romaine lettuce, onion, cucumbers and tomatoes and toss well.

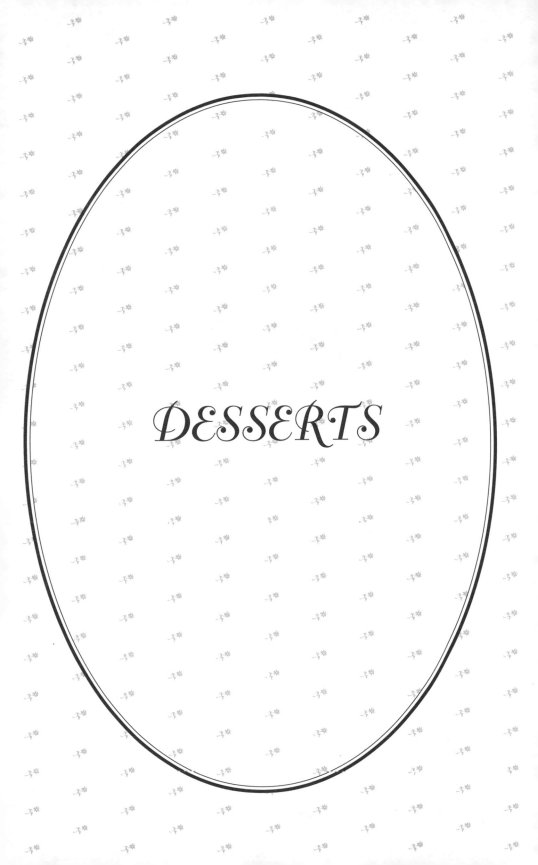

DESSERTS

St. Mary's Glacier

G uests of St. Mary's Glacier Bed and Breakfast enjoy country hospitality, freshly prepared gourmet breakfasts, the warmth of a roaring fire in the parlor or a hammock for two.

For a romantic getaway, two spacious suites feature king brass beds, whirlpool tubs and private decks with breathtaking mountain views. Two rooms with queen brass beds offer magnificent views of the Continental Divide.

INNKEEPERS:	*Jackie & Steve Jacquin*
ADDRESS:	*336 Crest Drive*
	Idaho Springs, CO 80452
TELEPHONE:	*(303) 567-4084*
ROOMS:	*5 Suites; All with private baths*
OPEN:	*Year-round*
CHILDREN:	*Not recommended*
ANIMALS:	*Prohibited*
SMOKING:	*Restricted to outdoor areas*

Bacardi Rum Cake

1 c. pecans or walnuts, chopped
1 pkg. (18 1/2 oz.) yellow cake mix (without pudding in the mix)
1 pkg. (3.4 oz.) Jell-O instant vanilla pudding mix
4 eggs
1/4 c. cold water
1/2 c. Wesson oil
1/2 c. Bacardi light or dark rum, 80 proof

Preheat oven to 325° F. Grease and flour 10-inch tube or 12-cup Bundt pan. Sprinkle nuts over bottom of pan. Mix all cake ingredients together. Pour batter over nuts. Bake about 1 hour. Cool for approximately 30 minutes and invert onto serving plate. (Make glaze while cake is cooling.) Prick all over top of cake with a toothpick. Drizzle and smooth glaze evenly over top and sides, allowing glaze to soak into cake. Keep spooning the glaze over cake until all glaze has been absorbed.

<u>Glaze</u>
1/4 lb. (1 stick) butter
1/4 c. water
1 c. sugar
1/2 c. Bacardi rum

Melt butter in a medium size saucepan. Stir in water and sugar. Boil for 5 minutes, stirring constantly. Remove from heat and cool slightly. Stir in rum <u>slowly</u>, so it doesn't splatter. While warm, spoon over cake.

Ambiance Inn

The Ambiance Inn is within walking distance of downtown Carbondale, a small mountain community located at the base of the Sopris Mountains. Breakfast is served daily in the dining room and although the meat and egg recipes vary, guests can always count on the freshly baked original breads.

Accommodations are superior, ranging from the Aspen Suite, Sonoma Room, Santa Fe Room and the Kauai Room, all with private baths and each with its own special "ambiance."

INNKEEPERS:	*Bob & Norma Morris*
ADDRESS:	*66 N. Second Street; Carbondale, CO 81623*
	PO Box 10932; Aspen, CO 81612
TELEPHONE:	*(970) 963-3597; (800) 350-1515*
ROOMS:	*4 Rooms; Private baths*
OPEN:	*Year-round*
CHILDREN:	*No restrictions*
ANIMALS:	*Extra charge for pets*
SMOKING:	*Restricted areas only*

Chocolate Carrot Cake

2 c. flour
1 1/2 c. sugar
1 c. salad oil
1/2 c. orange juice
1/4 c. cocoa
2 t. baking soda
1 t. salt
1 t. cinnamon
1 t. vanilla
4 eggs
2 c. shredded carrots
1 (4 oz.) pkg. shredded coconut
Glaze or icing (your favorite or try suggested recipe below)

In a large bowl, mix at low speed first ten ingredients. Mix until well blended, scraping often. Increase speed to high for 2 minutes. Stir in carrots and coconut. Spoon into greased and floured Bundt pan. Bake at 350° F. for 50-55 minutes, or until a toothpick comes out clean. Cool on wire rack about 10-15 minutes and remove from pan. Pour a glaze over or ice the cake.

> *Carol's Corner
> *Try this orange glaze on the chocolate carrot cake – it's a very nice complement.*
> *ORANGE GLAZE: Combine 1 cup powdered sugar with 2 tablespoons frozen orange juice concentrate (thawed) and 1/4 teaspoon grated orange peel (optional). Add some orange juice a few drops at a time until glaze consistency*

Logwood

L ogwood Bed and Breakfast is located 12 miles north of Durango and 13 miles south of Purgatory Ski Resort (just off the Million Dollar Highway 550) on the banks of the Animas River. All of the guest rooms have large picture windows and are attractively furnished with colorful home-stitched quilts to match the inn's western decor.

Throughout the day, award winning homemade desserts, fresh coffee, tea, hot chocolate, cider and soft drinks are available for guests.

INNKEEPERS:	*Debby & Greg Verheyden*
ADDRESS:	*35060 U.S. Highway 550 N.*
	Durango, CO 81301
TELEPHONE:	*(970) 259-4396; (800) 369-4082*
ROOMS:	*5 Rooms; 1 Suite; All with private baths*
OPEN:	*Year-round*
CHILDREN:	*No children under 8*
ANIMALS:	*Prohibited; Resident cats*
SMOKING:	*Prohibited*

Sour Cream Pound Cake

1 c. margarine or butter
3 c. sugar
6 large eggs
3 c. all-purpose flour
1/4 t. baking soda
1 (8 oz.) carton sour cream
1 t. vanilla flavoring
1 t. almond flavoring

Beat butter at medium speed about 2 minutes until soft and creamy. Gradually add sugar, beating about 5 minutes. Add eggs <u>two at a time</u>, beating until yellow disappears. Combine flour and baking soda. Add to creamed mixture alternately with sour cream. Mix at low speed after each addition. Stir in flavorings. Pour batter into greased and floured 10-inch tube pan. Bake at 325° F. for 1 hour and 20 minutes, or until <u>lightly</u> browned on top and toothpick comes out clean. Cool in pan on wire rack about 15 minutes and remove from pan. Finish cooling on wire rack.

"We are known for our wonderful country and gourmet breakfasts, but our cakes and cookies have won six awards. We are self-taught cooks (chefs) and love what we are doing. We are the only B&B on the Animas River and we are the only log home B&B in Durango."
Debby Verheyden – Logwood B&B

Silver Wood

Silver Wood Bed and Breakfast is a contemporary home set in rural Colorado. It is located near the prehistoric petrified trees of the Florissant Fossil Beds National Monument. Within a short distance is the cog railroad that guests can ride to the top of Pike's Peak.

Guests enjoy country gourmet breakfasts that are served in the dining room or on the east deck on warm sunny mornings. The varied menu includes decadent French toast, quiches and homemade breads.

INNKEEPERS:	*Larry & Bess Oliver*
ADDRESS:	*463 County Road 512*
	Divide, CO 80814
TELEPHONE:	*(719) 687-6784; (800) 753-5592*
ROOMS:	*2 Rooms; Both with private baths*
OPEN:	*Year-round*
CHILDREN:	*Children are welcome*
ANIMALS:	*Prohibited*
SMOKING:	*Prohibited*

Earthquake Cake

1 German chocolate cake mix
1 c. chopped pecans or walnuts
1 c. coconut
1/2 c. (1 stick) margarine, melted
1 (1 lb.) box powdered sugar
1 (8 oz.) pkg. cream cheese, softened

Spray a 9x13-inch pan with cooking spray. (At elevation of 9,200 feet, I find that a 8x15-inch pan works best. At lower elevations, the 9x13-inch pan will be full, but will not overflow.) Sprinkle nuts and coconut over bottom of pan. Prepare cake mix as directed on the box (in Colorado, be sure to make the high altitude adjustments shown on box). Pour cake batter over the nuts and coconut. Combine the margarine, powdered sugar and cream cheese. Mix well. Dollop this mixture over the top of the cake batter. Bake at 350° F. for 40-50 minutes, or until the top is solid. At high altitudes, bake at 375° F. for about 40-45 minutes. When done, the cake will have cracks, depressions, bumps and other odd formations to match the name, Earthquake.

> **Carol's Corner**
> An entertaining and very unique way to make a German chocolate cake!!! Kids, especially, will think this is great. Let your children or young guests watch through the oven glass door during the latter part of the baking time as the cake bubbles and oozes. And the bonus – it's as _delicious_ as it is _fun_!

"Breakfast is always determined by how the 'cook' feels when she sees the guests of the moment. I am a retired schoolteacher, and a background in chemistry enhances food choices and combinations. The Earthquake Cake recipe was given to me by my sister, Sue, who lives in 'earthquake country,' California."
Bess Oliver – Silver Wood B&B

Conejos Ranch

T he Conejos River, a fisherman's paradise, runs through the ranch. The soothing sound of the river helps guests relax, read, meditate or just ponder life.

The proprietor of the Conejos Ranch wrote about an evening when a little girl started crying. He asked, "What's wrong?" The little girl replied, "Tomorrow my family is leaving here and we <u>have</u> to go to Disney World!"

INNKEEPERS:	*Ms. Shorty Fry*
ADDRESS:	*25390 HWY 17*
	Antonito, CO 81120
TELEPHONE:	*(719) 376-2464*
ROOMS:	*8 Rooms; All with private baths; 6 Log Cabins*
OPEN:	*May-November; Calls taken year-round*
CHILDREN:	*Welcome*
ANIMALS:	*Welcome*
SMOKING:	*Allowed*

Praline Cheesecake
with Praline Sauce

Crust
1 1/4 c. crushed graham crackers (about 17)
1/4 c. granulated sugar
1/4 c. pecans, toasted
4-6 T. butter or margarine, melted

Combine cracker crumbs, sugar and pecans. Stir in margarine. Press into bottom and sides of 9-inch springform pan. Bake at 350° F. for 10 minutes.

Cheesecake
3 (8 oz.) pkg. cream cheese, softened
1 c. packed brown sugar
2 T. all-purpose flour
1 (5 1/3 oz.) can evaporated milk (or 2/3 cup)
1 1/2 t. vanilla
3 eggs
1/2 c. pecan halves, toasted

Mix cream cheese and brown sugar. Add flour, milk and vanilla; beat well. Add eggs and beat just until blended. Pour into baked crust. Bake at 350° F. for 50 minutes or until set. Cool in pan for at least 30 minutes. Loosen sides and remove rim from pan. (Don't worry if the top cracks; it will be covered by pecans and sauce.) Cool completely and arrange pecan halves on top of cake. Refrigerate cheesecake for several hours, or overnight is even better. Serve with warm Praline Sauce.

Praline Sauce
1 c. dark corn syrup
1/4 c. cornstarch
2 T. brown sugar
1 t. vanilla

Combine corn syrup, cornstarch and brown sugar. Cook until bubbly; then cook and stir for 2 minutes more. Remove from heat and add vanilla. Let sauce cool until it is just warm. Pour warm sauce over cheesecake. Serves 12-16. Note: The sauce can also be poured on the cheesecake and refrigerated and served completely chilled.

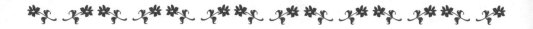

Lightner Creek Inn

D. COULTER

R esembling a French country manor, the Lightner Creek Inn is a luxury
mountain getaway for any season. Queen and king-size beds, down
comforters and cool mountain air assure guests of a peaceful night's rest.

Chosen as one of travel writer Doris Kennedy's favorite top ten inns in
Colorado, the Lightner Creek Inn sits on 6 acres of woodlands, meadows
and professionally landscaped flower gardens.

INNKEEPERS:	*Suzy & Stan Savage*
ADDRESS:	*999 C.R. 207*
	Durango, CO 81301
TELEPHONE:	*(970) 259-1226; (800) 268-9804*
ROOMS:	*10 Rooms; All with private baths*
OPEN:	*Year-round*
CHILDREN:	*Welcome*
ANIMALS:	*Prohibited*
SMOKING:	*Prohibited*

Frozen Oranges
with Raspberry Sauce

Large oranges (allow 1 orange per 2 servings)
Vanilla frozen yogurt
Granulated sugar
Whipped cream
Brown sugar

Cut oranges in half. Cut out center core. Scoop sections out and put in blender. Set aside orange shells. Add frozen yogurt and blend until creamy. Freeze yogurt mixture overnight. Roll orange shell halves in sugar and freeze overnight. Once frozen, scoop creamy mixture into orange shell. Top with Raspberry Sauce, whipped cream and a pinch of brown sugar.

<u>Raspberry Sauce</u>
1 c. fresh or frozen raspberries
1 T. honey
1/2 t. vanilla
1 t. cornstarch
1/8 c. water
Tiny pinch of salt

In a small saucepan, combine raspberries, honey and vanilla. Stir over low heat until just boiling. Mix cornstarch with water and salt and add to raspberries. Cook over low heat until thickened.

> **Carol's Corner**
> *This is a very pretty dessert! It could also be made with vanilla ice cream or try orange sherbet. If you don't care for the texture of orange pulp, you could still make this colorful dish by omitting the orange sections and filling the orange shells with plain frozen yogurt. Save the orange segments for another use (fruit salad, etc.). Tip: If the orange halves are not sitting flat on the serving plate, slice off a very small piece of the orange skin on the bottom of the shell.*

The Last Resort

The Last Resort Bed and Breakfast is nestled along the scenic banks of Coal Creek in the heart of downtown Crested Butte. This unique and convenient lodging experience features a private library, steam room, spacious solarium with magnificent mountain views, private Jacuzzis and an "all you can eat" hearty breakfast.

Extra amenities include guided cross-country and hiking tours. French and Spanish are spoken.

INNKEEPERS:	*Rita Wengrin*
ADDRESS:	*213 Third Street; PO Box 722*
	Crested Butte, CO 81224
TELEPHONE:	*(970) 349-0445; (800) 349-0445*
ROOMS:	*7 Rooms; Private and shared baths*
OPEN:	*Year-round*
CHILDREN:	*Children over 12 are welcome*
ANIMALS:	*Prohibited*
SMOKING:	*Prohibited*

Apple Walnut Delight

4 apples (any kind)
Cinnamon, to taste
Nutmeg, to taste
1/2 c. Bisquick
1 c. sugar
2 T. butter, cut into pieces
2 eggs
1/3 c. milk

<u>Streusel Topping</u>
1 c. Bisquick
1/2 c. walnuts, chopped
1/3 c. brown sugar
3 T. firm butter, cut into pieces

Peel and core the apples. Slice them into a greased 10-inch deep dish pie plate. Sprinkle some cinnamon and nutmeg over the apples and toss to combine. In a mixing bowl, beat together the Bisquick, sugar, butter, eggs and milk. Pour mixture over the apples. Combine the Streusel ingredients by hand and sprinkle it over batter and apples. Bake at 325° F. for about 1 hour. Serve with a dollop of whipped cream and a slice of apple for garnish. Equally good for breakfast or dinner. Serves 6-8.

> **Carol's Corner**
> *This is something similar to apple pie – except you don't have to make a crust! Try serving it warm with a big scoop of vanilla ice cream.*

Castle Marne

C astle Marne combines Old World elegance and Victorian charm with modern-day convenience and comfort. Each guest room is a unique experience in pampered luxury. Carefully chosen furnishings bring together authentic period antiques, family heirlooms, and exacting reproductions that create the mood of long-ago charm and romance.

Guests awaken to the spicy aroma of brewing Marne-blend coffee and homemade breads and muffins.

INNKEEPERS:	*Jim & Diane Peiker; Louis & Melissa Feher-Peiker*
ADDRESS:	*1572 Race Street*
	Denver, CO 80206
TELEPHONE:	*(303) 331-0621; (800) 92-MARNE*
ROOMS:	*8 Rooms; 1 Suite; All with private baths*
OPEN:	*Year-round*
CHILDREN:	*Not suitable for children under 10*
ANIMALS:	*Prohibited*
SMOKING:	*Prohibited*

Raspberry Truffles

1 c. (6 oz.) semisweet chocolate chips
2 squares (1 oz. each) unsweetened chocolate, chopped
1 1/2 c. powdered sugar
1/2 c. butter, softened
2 T. raspberry liqueur
Chocolate sprinkles, cocoa, nuts, or cookie crumbs (truffle coatings)

Melt the chocolate chips and unsweetened chocolate in a heavy small saucepan over low heat, stirring constantly. Set aside. In a bowl, combine the powdered sugar, butter and liqueur using an electric mixer. Beat in the cooled chocolate until smooth. Refrigerate about 30 minutes or until the mixture is fudgy and can be shaped into balls. Shape the mixture into 1-inch balls by rolling in the palms of your hands. Then roll the truffles in chocolate sprinkles, cocoa, chopped nuts or cookie crumbs to add flavor and prevent the truffle from melting in your fingers. Store in refrigerator until serving time. Makes about 34 truffles.

"For those on chocolate only diets!"
Diane Peiker – Castle Marne

Two Sisters Inn

The honeymoon cottage at Two Sisters Inn offers a white wicker bedroom with featherbed, gas log fireplace and a shower skylight to let in sunshine and moon beams.

"Check out the skylights . . . they'll bring you closer to Colorado's blue sky and its bright night stars."

~ *Sojourn Magazine*

INNKEEPERS:	*Wendy Goldstein & Sharon Smith*
ADDRESS:	*Ten Otoe Place*
	Manitou Springs, CO 80829
TELEPHONE:	*(719) 685-9684; (800) 2-SIS-INN*
ROOMS:	*4 Rooms; 1 Cottage; Private & shared baths*
OPEN:	*Year-round*
CHILDREN:	*Well-supervised children are welcome*
ANIMALS:	*Prohibited*
SMOKING:	*Prohibited*

Two Sisters' Gems
(Cherry Diamonds)

1 (5 oz.) pkg. dried cherries
1/4 c. Grand Marnier (or frozen orange juice concentrate, thawed)
1/2 c. butter or margarine, slightly softened
1/4 c. sugar
1 1/3 c. flour, divided
2 eggs
1 c. packed brown sugar
1/2 t. vanilla
1/2 t. baking powder
1/4 t. salt
1/2 c. coconut, shredded (preferably unsweetened)
1/2 c. chopped nuts

Preheat oven to 350° F. Put cherries in small saucepan with 1/3 cup water and Grand Marnier or orange juice. Simmer gently for 10 minutes. Remove from heat and cool in pan. Carefully check for pits; then chop and set aside. Blend together butter, sugar and 1 cup of the flour until crumbly. Pat into bottom of greased 8x8-inch or 9x9-inch square pan. Bake at 350° F. about 15 minutes, or until golden brown. Remove from oven. Beat eggs, brown sugar and vanilla until creamy. Sift remaining 1/3 cup flour with baking powder and salt, and blend into egg mixture. Stir in cherries, coconut and nuts. Spread over baked layer. Bake for approximately 30 minutes longer. Cool completely. Cut into diamonds. Makes 16 servings.

The Porter House

The Porter House Bed and Breakfast was originally built in the Queen Anne Victorian style by Dr. Frank Porter, a respected physician and surgeon in the Windsor community. The Windsor Leader newspaper reported, "Dr. Porter's magnificent residence is the prettiest house in northern Colorado."

The Porter House is the perfect setting for corporate retreats, business conferences, seminars, wedding receptions or any special occasion.

INNKEEPERS:	*Tom & Marni Schmittling*
ADDRESS:	*530 Main Street*
	Windsor, CO 80550
TELEPHONE:	*(970) 686-5793*
ROOMS:	*3 Rooms; 1 Suite; All with private baths*
OPEN:	*Year-round*
CHILDREN:	*Children 12 and older are welcome*
ANIMALS:	*Prohibited*
SMOKING:	*Prohibited*

Porter House Oatmeal Cranberry Cookies

1 c. butter (2 sticks), softened
1 c. brown sugar, firmly packed
2 eggs
2 c. flour
1 1/2 t. baking soda
2 c. oatmeal (old fashioned or quick)
1 1/2 c. dried cranberries
1 1/2 c. white chocolate chips
1/2 c. chopped walnuts (optional)

Beat together the butter and brown sugar. Add eggs and mix until combined. Stir in the flour, baking soda and oatmeal. Add the cranberries, chips and nuts. Use a cookie scoop for evenly sized cookies or drop by rounded tablespoon onto lightly greased baking sheet. Bake in preheated oven at 375° F. for 10-12 minutes. Let stand for about 2 minutes; remove to wire rack to cool completely. Makes about 7-8 dozen cookies.

Carol's Corner
Reach for one of these delicious cookies whenever you need a pick-me-up! These are one of Rod's favorites, only he usually takes more than one!!!

The Boulder Victoria

D.SPRINGER '90 ©

H ospitality is an art at The Boulder Victoria Historic Inn. Guests enjoy an abundant breakfast, served each morning in the bay-windowed dining room, on the spacious canopied patio or in the guest's room. Afternoon tea includes scones, lemon curd, shortbread and cakes.

The inn is located just two blocks from Boulder's Pearl Street Pedestrian Mall, home to fine dining, shopping and Boulder's thriving business community.

INNKEEPERS:	*Zoe Kircos*
ADDRESS:	*1305 Pine Street*
	Boulder, CO 80302
TELEPHONE:	*(303) 938-1300*
ROOMS:	*6 Rooms; 1 Suite; All with private baths*
OPEN:	*Year-round*
CHILDREN:	*Unable to accommodate children under 12*
ANIMALS:	*Prohibited*
SMOKING:	*Prohibited*

Kristen's Mocha Chip Cookies

2 1/2 c. semisweet chocolate chips, divided
1 c. butter, softened
1 c. brown sugar
1 c. granulated sugar
2 eggs
4 t. hot water
4 T. instant coffee granules
2 t. vanilla
3 c. flour
1 1/2 t. baking soda
1/2 t. salt
Powdered sugar

Melt 1 cup of the chocolate chips over low heat and set aside. In a large bowl, cream together butter, brown sugar and granulated sugar. Add the eggs and mix until smooth. Stir coffee granules into hot water until dissolved, and stir it into the butter mixture, along with the vanilla. Mix in melted chocolate. In small bowl, combine flour, baking soda and salt. Gradually stir this into the butter mixture. Blend in remaining 1 1/2 cups chocolate chips. Refrigerate dough until stiff. Preheat oven to 350° F. Form chilled dough into small balls, and roll in powdered sugar. Place on ungreased cookie sheet and bake for about 8-10 minutes. Remove from oven when surface appears "cracked" and dough has spread somewhat, but not yet flat. Especially yummy and chewy when served warm. Makes about 8 dozen.

> ❋ Carol's Corner
> *These are wonderful! Keep some in the freezer.*
> *Heated in the microwave for a few seconds, they*
> *taste like they were freshly baked.*

Meister House

Originally built in the late 1800's as a hotel, the Meister House Bed and Breakfast is located near the Upper Arkansas River Valley and the Collegiate Mountain Range. Guests enjoy the sunrise over Sleeping Indian Mountain while savoring a hearty gourmet breakfast.

Owners Frank and Barb enjoy cooking. Both were in the restaurant business before buying and renovating this unique bed and breakfast.

INNKEEPERS:	*Barbara & Frank Hofmeister*
ADDRESS:	*414 East Main Street; PO Box 1133*
	Buena Vista, CO 81211
TELEPHONE:	*(719) 395-9220; (800) 882-1821*
ROOMS:	*7 Rooms; All with private baths*
OPEN:	*Year-round*
CHILDREN:	*Children over the age of 10 are welcome*
ANIMALS:	*Prohibited*
SMOKING:	*Prohibited*

Meister House
Trail Mix Cookies

3/4 c. (1 1/2 sticks) butter, softened
3/4 c. sugar
3/4 c. packed light brown sugar
2 eggs
1 t. vanilla extract
2 c. flour
1 t. baking soda
1/2 t. cinnamon
1/2 t. salt
3 c. Trail Mix (use your favorite, or try the recipe below)

Heat oven to 350° F. In large bowl, cream butter and both sugars. Add eggs and vanilla. In small bowl, stir together flour, soda, cinnamon and salt. Stir trail mix into flour mixture. Gradually add flour mixture to butter mixture. Drop dough by spoonfuls on greased cookie sheet and bake for 10-15 minutes. Cool on wire racks. Makes about 4 dozen cookies.

Meister House Trail Mix
4 c. granola of your choice
1 1/2 c. dried cranberries
1 c. butterscotch chips
1 c. banana chips
1 c. raw pumpkin seeds

Mix all together. Note: This trail mix can be substituted for chocolate chips in any cookie recipe. Add 2 cups of the mix instead of the chips.

> **Carol's Corner**
> *Next time you are hiking in the mountains, take along some of these cookies or a bag of the trail mix in your backpack. A perfect snack for when you want to take a breather!*

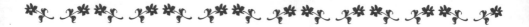

The Manor

The majestic mountains that surround The Manor Bed and Breakfast provide guests with some of the most spectacular hiking, mountain biking and Jeep trails that are accessible in Colorado. Guests can ski Telluride for half-price or soak in the hot springs for free.

The guest rooms are tastefully decorated with Victorian furnishings. Each of the seven rooms is located on the second or third floor, with commanding views of the surrounding mountains.

INNKEEPERS: *Joel & Diane Kramer*
ADDRESS: *317 Second Street; PO Box 745*
Ouray, CO 81427
TELEPHONE: *(970) 325-4574*
ROOMS: *7 Rooms; All with private baths*
OPEN: *Year-round*
CHILDREN: *No small children*
ANIMALS: *Prohibited*
SMOKING: *Prohibited*

Wholesome Wheatgerm Oatmeal Cookies

1 1/3 c. margarine
2 t. vanilla
2 c. brown sugar (can reduce to 1 cup for reduced calories)
2 eggs

In a very large bowl, cream the above ingredients. Then add:

2 c. all-purpose flour
1 1/2 t. salt
1 t. baking soda
1 1/2 c. wheat germ
1 t. cinnamon
4 1/2 c. oats
1 1/2 c. raisins

Mix together. For large cookies, spoon dough 2-inch size on a lightly greased cookie sheet. Bake in a preheated oven at 350° F. for 12-15 minutes or until golden brown. Makes 3 dozen large cookies (or 5-6 dozen smaller cookies). Store cookies in an airtight container.

Make-ahead tip: These cookies freeze well.

"Served at our afternoon tea, these nutty textured cookies are a favorite. They also pack well for our guests, who take advantage of the numerous hiking trails in the local San Juan mountains. A healthy treat!"
Diane Kramer – The Manor B&B

Logwood

Guests of Logwood Bed and Breakfast enjoy the glorious fall color change of the Colorado aspen trees. Other activities they enjoy include riding in a horse-drawn sleigh, soaking in the famous Trimble Hot Springs or taking Jeep rides into the magnificent Rocky Mountains.

"Delightful, lovely, attractive . . . they (guests) can only come away with wonderful memories . . . Just delicious chocolate sour cream cake."

~ National Bed & Breakfast Association

INNKEEPERS:	*Debby & Greg Verheyden*
ADDRESS:	*35060 U.S. Highway 550 N.*
	Durango, CO 81301
TELEPHONE:	*(970) 259-4396; (800) 369-4082*
ROOMS:	*5 Rooms; 1 Suite; All with private baths*
OPEN:	*Year-round*
CHILDREN:	*No children under 8*
ANIMALS:	*Prohibited; Resident cats*
SMOKING:	*Prohibited*

The Best Oatmeal and Sour Cream Chocolate Chip Cookie in the West

2 c. flour
1 t. baking soda
1/2 t. salt
1 c. rolled oats
1 1/4 c. light brown sugar
1 c. unsalted sweet butter, softened
2 eggs
1 t. vanilla
1/2 c. sour cream
12 oz. (2 c.) semisweet chocolate chips
12 oz. (2 c.) milk chocolate chips
1/4 c. raisins (coarse chopped)
3/4 c. dried cherries (during the holidays use dried cranberries)
3/4 c. walnuts, chopped

> **Carol's Corner**
> *If you like your cookies loaded with chocolate chips, these are for you! Fill the cookie jar and then watch them disappear!*

Sift flour, baking soda and salt together; stir in rolled oats. Set aside. In large bowl, cream together the sugar and butter until light and fluffy. Beat in eggs and vanilla. Stir sifted ingredients into creamed mixture until just combined. Mix in sour cream and stir until just blended. Stir in chocolate chips, raisins, dried cherries and nuts. Drop by heaping teaspoonfuls onto ungreased baking sheets, placing cookies 2 inches apart. Bake at 350° F. for 12-15 minutes, or until slightly browned around the edges. Allow to cool on cookie sheets for 5 minutes before removing to wire racks to cool completely. Makes about 5 1/2 dozen cookies.

Flynn's Inn

Nelson's Room at Flynn's Inn Bed and Breakfast, named after the original owner, Murdoch G. Nelson, has a Southwestern decor with a comfortable, full-sized sleigh bed. The Vineyard, the largest room, has an attached deck, private full bath with shower and Jacuzzi tub and a separate sitting area with king-sized bed.

The Innkeepers leave freshly baked cookies and a beverage on the bedside tables every evening for their guests.

INNKEEPERS:	*Colleen & Carie Conway*
ADDRESS:	*700 Remington*
	Fort Collins, CO 80524
TELEPHONE:	*(970) 484-9984*
ROOMS:	*3 Rooms; Private and shared baths*
OPEN:	*Year-round*
CHILDREN:	*Can't accommodate children under 10*
ANIMALS:	*Prohibited*
SMOKING:	*Prohibited in house; Smoking areas provided on porch and in backyard*

Gingersnip Cookies

3/4 c. shortening
1 c. packed brown sugar
1 egg
1/4 c. molasses
2 1/4 c. flour
2 t. baking soda
1/2 t. salt
1 t. ginger
1 t. cinnamon
1/2 t. cloves
Powdered sugar

Cream shortening, brown sugar, egg and molasses. Sift in dry ingredients, <u>except</u> for powdered sugar, and stir until blended. Form into small balls and roll in powdered sugar. Place on greased cookie sheet. Bake at 375° F. for about 10 minutes. Makes about 4 dozen cookies.

"These gingersnips taste like the hard gingersnap cookie but stay soft and chewy This is the one recipe we are continually asked for."
Colleen Conway – Flynn's Inn

1899 Bed and Breakfast Inn

1899 Bed and Breakfast Inn is located in LaVeta, a lovely small town south of the Navajo Trail in southern Colorado at the base of the Spanish Peaks and Sangre de Cristo Mountains. The area offers cross-country skiing, horseback riding, hiking, golfing and fishing.

The Inn is in the National Register of Historic places. Guests say it is just like going into "Grandma's house."

INNKEEPERS:	*Marilyn Schwarz Hall*
ADDRESS:	*314 Main Street; PO Box 372*
	LaVeta, CO 81055
TELEPHONE:	*(719) 742-3576*
ROOMS:	*5 Rooms; Private and shared baths; 1 Cottage*
OPEN:	*Weekends only (Year-round)*
CHILDREN:	*Welcome*
ANIMALS:	*Animals allowed in cottage only*
SMOKING:	*Prohibited*

Grandma's Molasses Cookies

1 c. Grandma's molasses
1/2 c. sugar
3 T. butter
3 T. shortening
2 T. milk
4 c. unbleached flour
1 t. soda
1 t. salt
1 t. cloves
1 t. cinnamon
1 t. nutmeg

In a large saucepan, heat molasses to boiling point. Add sugar, butter, shortening and milk. Slow boil until sugar is dissolved. Mix in sifted dry ingredients. Chill dough. When dough is easy to work, roll out on a floured bread board and roll VERY, VERY THIN. Cut dough with cookie cutters and place on a greased cookie sheet and bake in a 375° oven for 7-10 minutes. The dough does not spread when baking, so you can get a lot of cookies on a cookie sheet. Makes 4 dozen or more very thin, crisp cookies.

"I serve these at Christmas when the Art Guild and our Inn have the Belgian trolley pulled by draft horses. The carolers enjoy these when they come back for warm drinks and refreshments."
Marilyn Schwarz Hall – 1899 B&B Inn

Conejos Ranch

The hospitality, fine food and comfortable surroundings at the Conejos Ranch all contribute in bringing guests back year after year. The Ranch has a warm, rustic and inviting lodge that not only houses eight rooms, but also a den/sitting room that overlooks the grounds and river.

An outside deck provides a wonderful spot for guests to enjoy a cup of coffee or to reflect on the surrounding beauty.

INNKEEPERS: *Ms. Shorty Fry*
ADDRESS: *25390 HWY 17*
Antonito, CO 81120
TELEPHONE: *(719) 376-2464*
ROOMS: *8 Rooms; All with private baths; 6 Log Cabins*
OPEN: *May-November; Calls taken year-round*
CHILDREN: *Welcome*
ANIMALS: *Welcome*
SMOKING: *Allowed*

Conejos Cookies

1 c. butter
1 c. sugar
1 c. brown sugar
1 egg
1 c. vegetable oil
1 T. pure vanilla extract
1 c. rolled oats
1 c. Rice Krispies
1/2 c. shredded coconut
1/2 c. chopped toasted pecans
3 1/2 c. sifted all-purpose flour
1 t. baking soda
1 t. salt

Preheat oven to 325° F. Cream butter, sugar and brown sugar until light and fluffy. Add egg, vegetable oil and vanilla. Mix well. Add oats, Rice Krispies, coconut and pecans. Stir well. Add flour, soda and salt. Stir until well blended. Drop by teaspoonfuls on lined or greased insulated cookie sheets. Bake approximately 15 minutes. Makes 6 dozen.

"We make an attempt to have these in the rooms when our guests arrive! We also put them in our boxed lunches."
Janna Nall – Conejos River Ranch

Holden House - 1902

Resident owners Sallie and Welling Clark moved from California in 1985 and lovingly restored the neglected 1902 Victorian house and carriage house. In 1986 they began welcoming guests to share in their love of old homes.

"This inn is clearly one of the premier B&B's in the state."

Fawn Germer, *Rocky Mountain News*

INNKEEPERS:	*Sallie & Welling Clark*
ADDRESS:	*1102 W. Pikes Peak Avenue*
	Colorado Springs, CO 80904
TELEPHONE:	*(719) 471-3980*
ROOMS:	*2 Rooms; 4 Suites; All with private baths*
OPEN:	*Year-round*
CHILDREN:	*Prohibited*
ANIMALS:	*Prohibited; 2 Resident cats*
SMOKING:	*Prohibited*

Chocolate Chunk
White Chocolate Chip Cookies

3/4 c. brown sugar
3/4 c. butter or margarine
2 eggs
1 t. vanilla
2 1/2 c. flour
1 t. baking soda
6 oz. chocolate chunks
5 oz. Hershey's vanilla chips
1/4 c. chopped walnuts

Preheat oven to 375° F. Soften brown sugar and butter in microwave for one minute on high. Add eggs and vanilla. Add flour and baking soda to sugar/egg mixture. When well mixed, add chocolate chunks, vanilla chips and walnuts. Place by well rounded teaspoonfuls on ungreased insulated cookie sheet. Bake for 10-12 minutes or until slightly brown on top. Makes approximately 2 dozen cookies.

Carol's Corner
Chocolate chunks are sometimes hard to find. Substitute with chocolate chips or make your own chunks from semisweet chocolate baking bars. Be sure you use an insulated cookie sheet. It keeps the cookies from getting too brown on the bottom. I use the insulated cookie sheets for almost everything. Consider investing in one, if you haven't already.

"A favorite for afternoon tea. The Holden House's bottomless cookie jar is always a hit with our bed and breakfast guests."
Sallie Clark – Holden House 1902 B&B Inn

B & B
POTPOURRI

Romantic RiverSong Inn

The rooms at Romantic RiverSong Inn are named after wildflowers found in the Rocky Mountain region. All of the rooms have private baths, fireplaces and large tubs. Special honeymoon and romance packages are available. Wedding parties, including the bride and groom, must not exceed 12 individuals.

The Estes Park area offers special events that include a Scottish Festival, Rooftop Rodeo, Aspenfest and the Estes Park Spring Snow Festival.

INNKEEPERS:	*Gary & Sue Mansfield*
ADDRESS:	*PO Box 1910*
	Estes Park, CO 80517
TELEPHONE:	*(970) 586-4666*
ROOMS:	*9 Rooms; All with private baths*
OPEN:	*Year-round*
CHILDREN:	*Not suitable for children*
ANIMALS:	*Prohibited*
SMOKING:	*Outside only!*

Blueberry Vinaigrette

1/3 c. olive oil
1/3 c. blueberry syrup
1-2 t. honey
2 t. Dijon mustard
5 T. lime juice
Dash of cayenne pepper
Salt, optional

Combine all ingredients and shake vigorously. Refrigerate. A few minutes before serving time, remove vinaigrette from refrigerator and shake again. Makes about 1 cup.

Serving suggestion: Steam fresh asparagus spears until they are crisp-tender. On a serving plate, lay the spears in a crisscross fashion on top of a tomato slice. Sprinkle on a small amount of the vinaigrette. Very colorful!

Elizabeth Street Guest House

Guests awaken to the tantalizing aroma of freshly brewed coffee and homemade cinnamon apple muffins. The full breakfast includes tea, coffee, fruit, juice, pastries, cereals and such intriguing delights as Scotch Eggs or Dutch Babies with Apples.

For a special fee, in-town students, friends or business associates are welcome to join the Elizabeth Street guests for breakfast.

INNKEEPERS:	*John & Sheryl Clark*
ADDRESS:	*202 East Elizabeth Street*
	Ft. Collins, CO 80524
TELEPHONE:	*(970) 493-BEDS*
ROOMS:	*4 Rooms; Private and shared baths*
OPEN:	*Year-round*
CHILDREN:	*Welcome*
ANIMALS:	*Prohibited; Resident dog*
SMOKING:	*Prohibited*

Black Bean Dip

1 T. olive oil
1 or 2 cloves garlic, crushed
1 medium onion, chopped
2 (16 oz.) cans black beans, undrained
2 t. lime juice
1/4 t. oregano
1/4 t. salt
1/4 t. black pepper
1/2 t. cumin
1/4 t. coriander
1/4 t. sage
Dash of Tabasco sauce
Dollop of plain low fat yogurt

Heat oil in 2 quart saucepan. Sauté garlic and onion until translucent; add beans. Cook until liquid is reduced, but not evaporated. Add lime juice, spices and Tabasco sauce; continue cooking another 2 or 3 minutes. Add yogurt. Serve chilled with tortilla chips.

Note: Depending on the dip texture you prefer, the ingredients can be mixed with a fork, mashed with a fork or blended in a food processor.

Red Crags

Red Crags Bed and Breakfast is a magnificent, four-story Victorian mansion that has been known throughout the Pikes Peak area for over 120 years. The main house is 7,000 square feet and dominates the two-acre estate.

Once inside, guests marvel at the beautiful antiques, hardwood floors and high ceilings. The formal dining room, where a gourmet breakfast is served, features a rare cherry wood Eastlake fireplace.

INNKEEPERS:	*Howard & Lynda Lerner*
ADDRESS:	*302 El Paso Boulevard*
	Manitou Springs, CO 80829
TELEPHONE:	*(719) 685-1920; (800) 721-2248*
ROOMS:	*2 Rooms; 4 Suites; All with private baths*
OPEN:	*Year-round*
CHILDREN:	*No accommodations for children under 10*
ANIMALS:	*Prohibited*
SMOKING:	*Prohibited*

Grandma Kitty's Little Quiches

16 oz. small curd cottage cheese
4 oz. ricotta cheese
3 T. (heaping) sour cream
1/2 c. Bisquick
3 eggs, beaten
1/4 lb. (1 stick) butter, melted
8 oz. Swiss cheese, shredded

In a large bowl, mix together all ingredients. Spray mini muffin tins with vegetable spray. Using a pastry bag (or small spoon), fill muffin tins almost to the top. Bake at 350° F. for about 30 minutes. Let sit a couple minutes before gently removing from muffin tins. Serve immediately, or these may be frozen for later use. If frozen, pop them in the microwave for a minute or two to heat, and then serve.

Carol's Corner

These appetizers are good as is, or be creative – top with a 1/4 teaspoon of one of the following: picante sauce, Major Grey's Chutney, or a tangy mustard.

The Porter House

Guests of this beautifully restored 1898 Victorian Inn are transported back to a time where gracious living was predominant. Located in the "Tri-City Region" of Fort Collins, Greeley and Loveland, guests of The Porter House enjoy such pleasures as a walk to Lake Windsor, known for its diverse bird population.

All rooms have queen-sized beds, cable TV, luxurious terry robes, down filled comforters, central air conditioning and fresh cut flowers.

INNKEEPERS:	*Tom & Marni Schmittling*
ADDRESS:	*530 Main Street*
	Windsor, CO 80550
TELEPHONE:	*(970) 686-5793*
ROOMS:	*3 Rooms; 1 Suite; All with private baths*
OPEN:	*Year-round*
CHILDREN:	*Children 12 and older are welcome*
ANIMALS:	*Prohibited*
SMOKING:	*Prohibited*

Mediterranean Appetizer

Sun-dried tomatoes
Crusty French bread, sliced into 1/2-inch slices
Pesto sauce
Feta cheese
Greek calamata olives, pitted and thinly sliced
Parmesan cheese, freshly grated

Bring 2 cups of water to a boil. Submerge tomatoes in boiling water for 2 minutes to reconstitute. Drain the tomatoes, cut into slivers and set aside. Spread about a tablespoon of pesto sauce on each slice of bread. Sprinkle a tablespoon of crumbled feta cheese on top of the pesto sauce. Add 2 or 3 slices of Greek olives and the sun-dried tomatoes. Sprinkle with Parmesan cheese. Bake in a 425° F. oven for about 10 minutes, checking often to prevent burning. Serve hot.

"The hit of a party or gathering! We serve
them to our guests with wine in the evening."
Marni Schmittling – Porter House B&B Inn

Purple Mountain Lodge

P urple Mountain Lodge is nestled in the valley that is home to Crested Butte, Colorado. A light, cheerful atmosphere welcomes guests. Rooms are tastefully decorated with antiques and down comforters that are adorned with cheerful plaids, denims and bright floral duvet covers.

Marilyn and Paul Caldwell purchased the Purple Mountain Lodge in 1995. Since then, they've been busily refurbishing the B&B.

INNKEEPERS:	*Marilyn & Paul Caldwell*
ADDRESS:	*714 Gothic Avenue; PO Box 547*
	Crested Butte, CO 81224
TELEPHONE:	*(970) 349-5888; (800) 286-3574*
ROOMS:	*5 Rooms; Private and shared baths*
OPEN:	*Year-round*
CHILDREN:	*Call ahead*
ANIMALS:	*Prohibited*
SMOKING:	*Prohibited*

Spinach-Wrapped Chicken
with Curry Mayonnaise

2 whole chicken breasts
1 can regular-strength chicken broth
1/4 c. soy sauce
1 T. Worcestershire sauce
1 bunch fresh spinach
8 c. boiling water
Curry Mayonnaise (recipe below)

> **♣Carol's Corner**
> *Short of time? Using boneless tenderloins of chicken breasts cuts cooking time down to 10 minutes, and there is no de-boning. The chicken appetizers and dip can be prepared one day in advance.*

In a 10-inch pan, combine chicken breasts, chicken broth, soy and Worcestershire sauce. Bring to a boil over medium heat; cover and reduce heat. Simmer until chicken is fork-tender, about 15 to 20 minutes. Lift chicken from broth and let cool slightly. Remove and discard skin and bones, then cut meat into 1-inch chunks. Wash spinach. Remove and discard stems. Place whole leaves in colander. Pour boiling water over leaves; drain thoroughly, then set aside to cool. To assemble: Place a chicken chunk at stem end of a spinach leaf. Roll over once, fold leaf in on both sides, and continue rolling around chicken. Secure end of leaf with a wooden pick. Serve with Curry Mayonnaise for dipping.

Curry Mayonnaise
1/4 c. mayonnaise
1/4 c. sour cream
2 t. curry powder
2 T. chopped Major Grey's chutney
1 t. grated orange peel

Mix all ingredients until smooth. Cover and refrigerate for at least 1 hour. Makes about 2/3 cup.

Woodland Inn

Guests of the Woodland Inn relax in the parlor that overlooks the peaceful woodlands where elk feed in the winter and hummingbirds visit in the summers. Breakfast is served fireside in the dining room. Guests may use the outdoor grill or walk to local restaurants for lunch or dinner.

Amenities include soft terry robes for each guest, coffee service for in-room enjoyment in the morning and a portable TV/VCR for private viewing.

INNKEEPERS: *Frank & Nancy O'Neil*
ADDRESS: *159 Trull Road*
Woodland Park, CO 80863
TELEPHONE: *(719) 687-8209; (800) 226-9565*
ROOMS: *7 Rooms; All with private baths; 1 Room available for disabled persons*
OPEN: *Year-round*
CHILDREN: *Children with well-behaved parents are welcome*
ANIMALS: *Resident dog and cat*
SMOKING: *Permitted outdoor only*

Tortilla Swirls

1 (8 oz.) pkg. cream cheese
1 (4 oz.) can chopped green chiles
Pimento, black olives, or radishes, chopped (optional)
3 flour tortillas
Garnish of choice

Place cream cheese in a medium size microwave safe bowl. Microwave for 30-40 seconds to soften cheese. Stir in chiles; mix well. If you wish, add any of the optional ingredients for color and pizzazz! Spread mixture onto flat tortillas and roll tightly (jelly roll style). Wrap rolled tortillas in plastic wrap and refrigerate for at least an hour. When ready to serve, remove from refrigerator and slice into 1-inch pieces. Lay the pieces on a plate with garnish, and serve as an appetizer.

"We send the Tortilla Swirls along as part of the 'Field Breakfast' for the pilot and crew of our hot air balloon, 'HIGH TIME.' Frank's balloon was given its name (by me) because it was 'high time' he got it! He had been flying for 8 years before he had his own balloon. Guests at the Woodland Inn Bed & Breakfast may join the festivities through our 'Crew Package' special."
Nancy O'Neil – Woodland Inn B&B

Mt. Sopris Inn

The Mt. Sopris Inn sits on 14 acres above the Crystal River. A bald eagle and peregrine falcon preserve are within view as is the Perry Ranch, one of the oldest working ranches in Colorado. A nearby fish hatchery produces rainbow trout for the area's rivers.

The breakfast table is set with bone china. Guests enjoy such tasty morning treats as Eggs Benedict and whole grain pancakes.

INNKEEPERS:	*Barbara Fasching*
ADDRESS:	*0165 Mt. Sopris Ranch Road; PO Box 126*
	Carbondale, CO 81623
TELEPHONE:	*(970) 963-2209; (800) 437-8675*
ROOMS:	*14 Rooms; All with private baths*
OPEN:	*Year-round*
CHILDREN:	*Not welcome*
ANIMALS:	*Prohibited*
SMOKING:	*Prohibited*

Wink's Chili Dip

1 (3 oz.) pkg. cream cheese, softened
1 (4 oz.) can green chilies, chopped
4 green onions, finely chopped
1 (15 oz.) can chili con carne (no beans)
1 (4 1/2 oz.) can black olives, chopped
3/4 c. Monterey Jack cheese, grated

Combine all ingredients and place in a round 8-inch or 9-inch pan. Bake at 325° F. for 40 minutes. Serve with lime 'n chile flavored restaurant style tortilla chips.

> ✿ Carol's Corner
>
> *For a quick snack or lunch, spread 1-2 tablespoons of any leftover Wink's Chili Dip on a flour tortilla. Sprinkle on a little bit of shredded cheese and heat in the microwave for 45 seconds (or until cheese melts). Top it with some shredded lettuce, chopped onion and tomato, and a spoonful of picante sauce. Roll it all up and you've made a " Quick as a Wink Burrito." Easy and delicious!*

Red Crags

The Teddy Roosevelt Suite at Red Crags, named for President Roosevelt who was a frequent visitor, is the premier honeymoon suite. It is furnished with a king-sized bed with feather mattress, ornate fireplace and sitting area where guests enjoy picturesque views of Pikes Peak and Colorado Springs.

Local areas of interest include the Air Force Academy, Cave of the Winds, Miramont Castle, Seven Falls and the Olympic Training Center.

INNKEEPERS:	*Howard & Lynda Lerner*
ADDRESS:	*302 El Paso Boulevard*
	Manitou Springs, CO 80829
TELEPHONE:	*(719) 685-1920; (800) 721-2248*
ROOMS:	*6 Suites; All with private baths*
OPEN:	*Year-round*
CHILDREN:	*Not suitable accommodations for children under 10*
ANIMALS:	*Prohibited; Resident dog*
SMOKING:	*Prohibited*

Zucchini Squares

4 eggs, slightly beaten
1/2 c. vegetable oil
3 c. zucchini, <u>thinly</u> sliced (about 3 or 4 small zucchini)
1 c. Bisquick
1/2 c. onion, finely chopped
1/2 c. Parmesan cheese
2 T. snipped parsley
1/2 t. salt
1/2 t. oregano
Dash pepper
1 clove garlic, finely chopped
1/4 t. Grey Poupon dijon mustard

Combine all ingredients. Pour into greased 9x13-inch baking pan. Bake at 350° for 25-35 minutes. It should be lightly browned, but do not overbake. Cut into small squares and serve as an appetizer.

> **Carol's Corner**
> *This could also be cut into individual serving size pieces and lightly sprinkled with paprika and freshly grated Parmesan cheese. Paired with a colorful fruit or lettuce salad, it would make a nice lunch.*

Scrubby Oaks

Scrubby Oaks Bed and Breakfast is located on 10 acres that overlook the Animas Valley and surrounding mountains. Family antiques, art works and fine books help create a quiet, country ambiance. Lovely patios and gardens surround the inn.

Gift items available in the "trading post" include sandcast Southwestern candles, pots by Van Emery, Southwestern key racks and coffee mugs and wine and pilsner glasses with the Scrubby Oaks logo.

INNKEEPERS: *Mary Ann Craig*
ADDRESS: *1901 Florida Road; PO Box 1047*
Durango, CO 81302
TELEPHONE: *(970) 247-2176*
ROOMS: *7 Rooms; Private and shared baths*
OPEN: *Last weekend in April through October*
CHILDREN: *Welcome*
ANIMALS: *Prohibited*
SMOKING: *Prohibited*

Jezebel Sauce

Great served over cream cheese with crackers.

1 (18 oz.) jar apricot-pineapple preserves
1 (18 oz.) jar apple jelly
1 (1.75 oz.) can dry mustard
1 (5 oz.) jar horseradish
1 T. cracked peppercorns

Combine all ingredients in a blender. Pour into an airtight container and store in refrigerator. To serve, spoon some sauce over an 8 oz. block of cream cheese as a spread for crackers. It is equally good served over roast beef or roast pork. Makes about 4 cups.

> **Carol's Corner**
> *Hang on to your hats for this one! It's a very tangy, sweet and spicy mustard sauce. Sure to be a hit!*

Mt. Sopris Inn

O riginally the home of a famed Aspen Skiing Corporation president, Mt. Sopris Inn is located on fourteen acres with panoramic views of Mt. Sopris, McClure Pass, Chair Mountain and overlooks the Crystal River. The two-story lobby entrance features a unique log and rail staircase, and the Great Room has a floor-to-ceiling fireplace.

A nature hiking path allows access to the Crystal River where guests can fish in one of the finest stream fishing areas in the Rocky Mountains.

INNKEEPERS:	*Barbara Fasching*
ADDRESS:	*0165 Mt. Sopris Ranch Road; PO Box 126*
	Carbondale, CO 81623
TELEPHONE:	*(970) 963-2209; (800) 437-8675*
ROOMS:	*14 Rooms; All with private baths*
OPEN:	*Year-round*
CHILDREN:	*Not welcome*
ANIMALS:	*Prohibited*
SMOKING:	*Prohibited*

Non-Alcoholic Sparkling Christmas Punch

4 c. apple juice
6 whole cardamom pods, broken
4 sticks cinnamon
1 t. vanilla
2 (12 oz.) bottles lemon-lime carbonated water, chilled
1 large red apple, cored and sliced crosswise
1/2 c. cranberries
Cheesecloth (for spices)

Heat apple juice. Place spices in cheesecloth bag and add to juice. Bring juice to a boil; reduce heat and simmer 5 minutes. Discard spice bag and chill juice. At serving time, pour juice into a large punch bowl. Stir in vanilla, carbonated water, apple slices and cranberries. Add ice.

Annabelle's

A nn, the owner, wrote the following story about how Annabelle's became a bed and breakfast.

Tim, Ann's husband, was in Norway on business while she recovered from knee surgery. Her father came from Virginia to help. While he was there, she told him how she had wanted to turn the two-bedroom, downstairs apartment into a B&B. After Ann's knee healed, she and her father remodeled the apartment. When Tim arrived home she said, "Welcome to Annabelle's Bed and Breakfast!"

INNKEEPERS:	*Tim & Ann Mealey*
ADDRESS:	*276 Snowberry Way*
	Dillon, CO 80435
TELEPHONE:	*(970) 468-8667*
ROOMS:	*3 Rooms; Two form a suite*
OPEN:	*Year-round*
CHILDREN:	*Children under 12 are FREE! (In their parent's room)*
ANIMALS:	*Prohibited*
SMOKING:	*Prohibited*

Kids' Recipes

Monster Toast
Put some **milk** in several small cups and add a different color of **food coloring** to each. Make sure the milk paint is bright! Using paintbrushes, let the kids paint their piece of **bread**. When they are done painting, lightly toast the bread. **Butter** the toast, if desired.

Fruit Kabobs
Cut up various **fruits**: Banana, apple, melon, etc. Cube some **cheese**, too. Put them on skewers and dip in **orange juice** and roll in **coconut**.

Sunshine Salad
Mix **1/2 carton plain yogurt** with **1 t. honey**. Put **1 slice pineapple** in each dish. Put 1 T. yogurt mixture in the middle. Eat the SUNSHINE!

Imagination Pancakes
Using regular **pancake batter**, swirl the batter around when you put it on the griddle or skillet. Let the kids tell you what it is!

Orange Julius
1 (6 oz.) can frozen orange juice concentrate
1 t. vanilla
1 3/4 c. water
12 ice cubes
1/4 c. sugar
1/2 c. dry milk
Combine all ingredients in a blender and serve. **Note: 1 1/2 cups fresh fruit** (bananas, strawberries, etc.) may be substituted for the concentrate.

"At Annabelle's B&B we specialize in families with children, since we have 3 boys of our own. We've been running a B&B for 4 years; our boys are now ages 3, 5 and 8. Here are a few recipe ideas for kids to eat!"
Ann Mealey – Annabelle's B&B

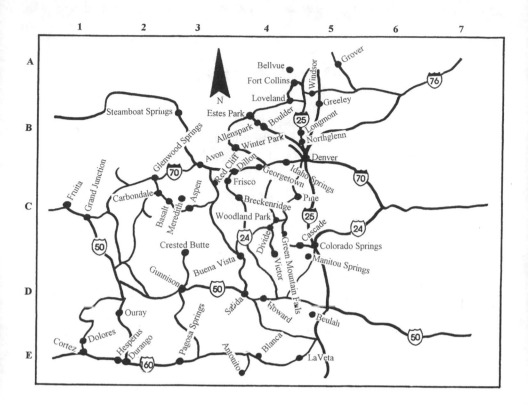

B&B Locations

Alphabetical Listing of Bed & Breakfasts

Index of Recipes

307

About the Authors

Carol McCollum Faino was born and raised in Des Moines, Iowa. She graduated from the University of Iowa and taught one year before marrying her high school sweetheart, Rod Faino, a navy pilot. Her new "career" as a Navy Officer's wife included raising two sons and a daughter and moving twelve times in the subsequent twenty-seven years. These frequent moves have given Carol the opportunity and challenge to teach in seven states, working with children from preschool age through high school. Carol, her husband, and younger son moved to the Denver area in 1992.

Doreen Kaitfors Hazledine grew up on a ranch in South Dakota and attended a one-room schoolhouse. She was a teacher and businesswoman before a serious illness changed the course of her life. When her health improved, she attended writing classes and screenwriting seminars. One of her screenplays is presently in development. Doreen and her husband, Don, live in Denver, Colorado.

PEPPERMINT PRESS

PO Box 370235
Denver, CO 80237-0235
1 (800) 758-0803
EMAIL: bbcookbook@aol.com
WEBSITE: www.bbcookbook.com

Please send me _____ copies of
COLORADO BED & BREAKFAST COOKBOOK

Each copy	$18.95	_____
S/H ($2.00 per additional copy)	$ 3.00	_____
CO residents add sales tax per copy	$ 1.38	_____
	TOTAL	_____

Make check payable to: **Peppermint Press**
(Payable in U.S. dollars only. Please no C.O.D.s or Cash.)

Name _____

Address _____

City _____ State _____ Zip _____

Phone number _____

Please charge to my VISA ___ or MC ___
Card number _____
Expiration date _____

Cardholder's signature _____

PEPPERMINT PRESS

PO Box 370235
Denver, CO 80237-0235
1 (800) 758-0803
EMAIL: bbcookbook@aol.com
WEBSITE: www.bbcookbook.com

Please send me _____ copies of
COLORADO BED & BREAKFAST COOKBOOK

Each copy	$18.95	_____
S/H ($2.00 per additional copy)	$ 3.00	_____
CO residents add sales tax per copy	$ 1.38	_____
	TOTAL	_____

Make check payable to: **Peppermint Press**
(Payable in U.S. dollars only. Please no C.O.D.s or Cash.)

Name _____

Address _____

City _____ State _____ Zip _____

Phone number _____

Please charge to my VISA ___ or MC ___
Card number _____
Expiration date _____

Cardholder's signature _____

PEPPERMINT PRESS
PO Box 370235
Denver, Colorado 80237-0235

MAILING LABEL - PLEASE PRINT

Name
Address
City & State
Zip Code

PEPPERMINT PRESS
PO Box 370235
Denver, Colorado 80237-0235

MAILING LABEL - PLEASE PRINT

Name
Address
City & State
Zip Code

I would like to have the following
stores / shops in my area handle
COLORADO BED & BREAKFAST COOKBOOK:

Store Name_____

Address_____

City_____ State_____Zip_____

Store Name_____

Address_____

City_____ State_____Zip_____

I would like to have the following
stores / shops in my area handle
COLORADO BED & BREAKFAST COOKBOOK:

Store Name_____

Address_____

City_____ State_____Zip_____

Store Name_____

Address_____

City_____ State_____Zip_____